Zero to Diamond:

Become a Million Dollar Real Estate Agent

Ricky Carruth

For Karlin

Zero to Diamond Publishing
Orange Beach, Alabama

Zero to Diamond:

Become a Million Dollar Real Estate Agent

Foreword

As I look back over the last decade and a half of my real estate career—especially the last three and a half years in which I consistently made over $50,000 every month and over 100 sales every year—I decided it was time to give back to the real estate community and unleash the basic principles that eventually molded me into the highly successful agent that I have become. Real estate changed my life and it can change yours as well. It gives you the opportunity to reach for the sky and create the kind of life you want instead of a life controlled by the ever-dreaded fixed paycheck. Real estate gives you choices and freedoms that are rarely found today.

In today's world, 90% of the wealth is controlled by the top 3% of the population. In real estate, it is said, 80% of transactions are handled by only the top 20% of active agents. Sounds lopsided, doesn't it? What separates the top end of success? How did they get there? How do I get there? These are the questions that future top producers should start to ask themselves.

As with success in all aspects of life and business, it all starts in your mind. It's mental. You must have the vision and the action: watching your future self achieve the largest of goals in your mind years before actually achieving them, and then doing the daily actions that lead to those accomplishments—those are the two main recipes for success. Seeing it and then doing it. You must have a vision and a reason to be successful. Without that, you are just floating in the wind.

For the super-achievers, it's a never-ending game of cat and mouse. A mouse is your new goal in life. Once caught, a new one emerges. Therefore, you are constantly trying new ideas and expanding your game to catch the next mouse.

The same applies in real estate. Your first mouse, or goal, is just to close one transaction. Once you achieve that, you create a new goal of closing your second transaction. Then one transaction per month. Then two per month. So on and so forth. Each time your goal changes, so will your attitude and motivation. Slowly, you are molding yourself into a highly-successful real estate agent, one day and one goal at a time.

I see agents all the time that have everything it takes to be a top producer. They are motivated, hard-working, smart, personable, etc. I can see it in their eyes that they will make it. The problem is that even if an agent is the one out of five who survives his/her first year in this business, it still takes years to gain the experience needed to understand what is behind consistent success in real estate.

Regardless of how motivated you may be, understand that it will still take years of hard work and frustration before you reach the top. However, the top is worth every second it takes to get there. To complete the transformation from non-producer to top producer, you must stay motivated and continue upgrading your skills and goals every step of the way. Don't dismiss this as clichéd information. This is the way you *must* think to become a top producer.

When I sat down to write this book, my goal was to make it as short and as powerful as possible. I did not want to write a long, tedious book that takes weeks to read. I want my readers to be able to take my system and run with it quickly. Time is money and the quicker I can relay my message to you, the quicker you can use these principles to make more sales.

They say that preparation is half the battle. While there is truth to that, don't get stuck in the preparation process.

Many agents spend their entire career trying to learn how to become a top producer, but never actually apply a fraction of what they have learned.

They never really get started. *Reaching for higher education in your field is a key to continued growth, but you must understand where the fine line is between *learning* and *taking action*.

*When I first started selling real estate, I had no website, no business cards, and no knowledge of how to sell property. That did not stop me from getting on the phone with hundreds of potential customers and sending mail-outs to future clients. Sure, I did eventually get a website and business cards.*The point is that I did not wait...I acted.

*There are two forms of education: the education you can get from research and reading, and the kind you get from experience. It takes a combination of both to succeed. Education, experience, action—you can't ignore any one of these three elements anymore than you could leave out a main ingredient in a cake recipe and still have a cake. *Becoming a million-dollar agent is exactly the same as baking a cake. Follow the recipe. This is very important, and I want you to understand what this means.

When you finish this book, you will have all the knowledge needed to become the top-producing agent in your office and even your entire market area. However, you may still lack experience. So you must take action; you can't just touch your toe to the pool, you must dive in headfirst. Yes, you will make mistakes. Don't let your fear of mistakes hold you back from being successful.

*The more experience you have, the more confidence you will build and the less fear you will have.

Learning from your mistakes is just as important, if not more important, than learning ways to become successful. Once you have knowledge *and* experience, then you will be on the right track to becoming a multimillion-dollar producer.

I encourage you to dive into the information you find in this book and go with it! Good luck and let me know if I can help you.

I still actively sell real estate and will never quit. It is what I was born to do. I also have a huge desire to help other real estate agents succeed. You can always contact me via my website at **www.ZeroToDiamond.com** where I also encourage you to take the online course, *Zero to Diamond: Become a Million-Dollar Real Estate Agent*. The course includes the *Zero to Diamond Action Plan* and *Zero to Diamond Membership*, which means I will personally call you to answer any questions you may have, and to help you develop a personalized business plan for achieving your real estate goals. I look forward to hearing from you. I am on a personal mission to help as many real estate agents achieve success as I can.

Like us on Facebook:

www.Facebook.com/ZeroToDiamond

Follow me on **Snapchat and Instagram @rickycarruth**.

And subscribe to my YouTube channel, *Ricky Carruth* (just type my name in the YouTube search window). I am always posting new content helping agents understand what it takes to succeed in this business.

~~~

Introduction

This book is divided into three main sections.

I. The first section focuses on the *mindset* of a million-dollar real estate agent.

II. The second section focuses on the *actions* of a million-dollar real estate agent.

III. The third section focuses on how to *maintain* this high level of success for years to come.

I felt it was best to break it down into three sections, with ideas grouped together in ways that will help you fully understand what I am trying to convey. The information I share, as a whole, is not found in any other book or recited by any other speakers out there. I've gathered these principles over the last few decades of my career. Everything contained in this book came from either a lesson learned by failure or by a huge success. These are all my failures and successes wrapped up for you to read and learn from.

This book offers you a clear plan to become the highest producing agent in your office and even your entire market, if you choose to use it. If not, that is okay, too. Not everyone wants to be the highest producer. However, if you take what I tell you and understand the principles shared, you could very well triple and quadruple your income over the next few years. I did! And if I can do it, I guarantee you that you can as well.*All it takes is a little dedication and hard work. So, get to reading and enjoy.

Thanks for your interest and support.

~~~

Section I:

The Philosophy of a Top Producing Real Estate Agent

1: Set Your Sails

Real estate success might as well be the unattainable Eighth Wonder of the World, the way that some agents perceive it. The problem is that half the agents make it much harder than it should be and the other half want to skip all the years of hard work and go straight to being a top producer in their first month.

Neither misperception works. Sure, you may get a quick deal or two early in your career, and if that happens, then congratulations. However, don't let those deals go to your head, don't think that you have mastered the real estate mountain and that it's all downhill from there. This business is as unforgiving as the weather on Mount Everest. It can slap you in the face and throw you back to the bottom in a heartbeat. It has a mind of its own and controls its own destiny. Beware.

Another metaphor: think of real estate as a sailboat lost at sea. It flows where the wind and current take it. No destination. No journey. When you get your real estate license, you are now the captain of the sailboat. You are thrown into the middle of the sea with a sailboat that doesn't know which way it's going, nor its final destination. It is up to you to learn how to work the sails against the wind and steer the boat through the current to start heading in the right direction.

In the beginning, it will take time to learn the process, to develop the habits of what to do and what not to do. And sometimes you will start heading in the right direction just long enough to get the feeling of success only to get thrown off course again and again. Until, one day after years and years of consistent hard work and lessons learned, it hits you: the sails are full, the rudder is working. You finally get it! And just like that, your sailboat starts heading in the right direction.

The right direction can be different for each of us. It's up to you to decide what direction you want to sail. For me, the goal was to have consistent closings every single month. This is the greatest challenge for most agents. This should be a goal for any full-time agent. Typically, after several years in the business, most good agents do plenty of deals, but they come in waves. One month will yield plenty of closings, the next month, zero.

✳ Even very seasoned agents still have a hard time realizing the actual reason why some agents have closings consistently month after month. They can't figure out what the secret technique is that creates consistent sales. Looking high and low, they search, read, and listen. Trying to learn what to do and how to do it, the agents bark up every tree they can find. After running into brick wall after brick wall, they finally hit something that makes a little sense. Once they find success, they continue using that same technique over and over to find that it works. Now momentum is starting to move in their direction.

Once momentum starts, you can't let it die.✳Momentum is the greatest force in real estate. You must learn how to use it to your advantage and never allow it to slow down. It's like pushing a truck. It's tough to get it moving, but once it is moving, it's easy to keep it going… unless you allow it to stop, whereupon you must start all over again.

Once the truck is moving at a good pace, it's time to change gears, to push a little harder and take it to another level. When the truck has reached top speed, the only thing that might slow you down is your personal stamina level.

*How bad do you want it? How long and hard will you push? Will you ever give up? For me: Never. I have been pushing for almost two decades now and don't see an end in sight.

Some agents don't have enough stamina to last a day in this business. Literally, not one day. I have seen it time and time again. Do you have the stamina it takes to push momentum higher and higher for decades? That's what it takes. That is the real question you should ask yourself.

Or are you looking for the easy path to success through a website or some "magical" huge deal that will make you rich? I will be very blunt about this: *There is absolutely no easy path to success in real estate. There is only one path.
*It's an uphill path of hard, consistent, honest work. And I can sum up the secret to having closings every month into a single idea, philosophy, or lifestyle. Here it is:

Consistent closings come from consistently creating and maintaining strong, long-lasting relationships with property owners who own property in the niche market you choose to sell in.

This single sentence should be written down and posted where you can see it every day. This is what everything you do day in and day out should be focused around. Let's dissect it and lay out the details behind what it means.

Look at the first part of the sentence, *"Consistent closings come from consistently...."* This is important because it stresses a principle: *if you want something consistently, you must do the activities that produce that result consistently. It's a chain reaction.

If you do what creates closings every single day, then soon enough you will start having closings every single month.
*Consistency is the key. You can't complain about not having consistent closings if you are not doing the activities

that produce closings on a consistent basis. This means you must work hard every day and focus on the activities that produce closings.

The next part of the sentence says, *"creating and maintaining strong, long-lasting relationships."* This is the activity that produces closings that you should be doing every day. Creating relationships with new clients and maintaining the relationships you created in the past is your most important job as an agent.*Every single closing that has ever been completed in the history of real estate has come from a relationship that an agent created and maintained. There is no way around this. Even if you write an offer the first hour you meet a buyer, this is still a relationship you *created* and are now *maintaining*.

*Your entire business must focus around creating and maintaining strong, long-lasting relationships. When I go to work in the morning, my job is *relationships*... not to do a transaction. Transactions are not the goal. Relationships are the goal.*Transactions come and go but relationships are forever. Think of a *transaction* as plucking a single apple from a tree; think of a *relationship* as planting an apple tree, fertilizing and nurturing its growth.*A relationship will bring you a hundred times more fruit than a transaction. *Transactions are the *byproduct* of the relationships you have developed.*The more relationships you have in place, the more transactions you will close.*This is the real root of real estate success. Mastering the relationship part of the business and realizing how many relationships you must have in place to achieve your goals is the big secret that all agents want to know and it's right in front of their noses. *Real estate is that simple.*

The last part of the sentence/principle states, *"with property owners who own property in the niche market you choose to sell in."* This refers to exactly which group of people you want to target to absolutely dominate your market and become the highest producing agent in your area.

Of course, we can create and maintain relationships with all kinds of people we already know, and I want you to follow those random relationships and see where they take you. However, if you want to completely take over your market and exceed your competition, you must work with the highest quality prospects in your market: property owners.

So, what makes property owners the highest quality prospect in any market? Answer: those are the prospects who produce the highest amount of commissions in the least amount of time possible. This is true for a variety of reasons. One reason: you don't spend as much time with them educating them on property ownership. You don't have to explain to them the responsibilities and costs of being an owner because they already own property, and therefore they know firsthand all the pros and cons of ownership.

With a first-time buyer, you must explain taxes, insurance, utilities, etc., as well as hundreds of other questions that a current owner will not ask. So, with a property owner, you can cut out the time spent educating. Also, a property owner can become a buyer or a seller at any moment if they so choose. This gives you two possibilities to pursue as opposed to just one. Putting yourself in the position to deal with prospects with more than one option to create a deal is far more efficient and productive than working with a prospect who can only complete one type of transaction. Do you agree? Take full advantage of this opportunity.

Also, if the property owner decides they want to buy, they usually know what they want. This makes it easier to find a property for them, versus a first-time buyer who may spend days with you looking at various properties all over the county, unsure of what they are looking for.

The bottom line is that strictly dealing with property owners as clients is the absolute most-efficient way to spend your time over all other prospects. Period.

So, set your sails in the direction of your goals. Work hard every day to create and maintain more and more relationships with the right people. Learn from your mistakes and reach for the sky. We want to dominate our market and outpace the competition… respectfully. We all must work with each other. Be respectful and professional with the other agents in your market. Consistently do the things that other agents aren't willing to do.

Once you get to a point where you feel comfortable in your business, that's when it's time to turn up the heat and keep pushing that truck to the next higher gear. Don't lose momentum. Don't give yourself any reason to slow down. This energetic, upbeat attitude should be embraced for the long-term. Stay positive and keep moving forward… with patience. Remember, Rome wasn't built in a day.

2: Success is a Lifestyle

In the beginning of the career of a top producer, agents are told to *Fake it 'til ya make it*. This is an old cliché that if used correctly can be very powerful. *Fake it 'til you make it* is a mentality that means *have no fear*. Dive right in headfirst and pretend like you do this every day—even if it's your first day in real estate. Having the ability to adapt to your surroundings quickly is important.

Once you begin to gain experience and know-how, you will feel more confident, and you'll know it's time to stop faking it. You can only fake it for so long before people figure you out. Once you *make it*, you must prove to everyone that being a highly successful agent is truly you—by adopting the *lifestyle* of a top producer.

As you jump into your real estate career, immediately **pay attention to the top producers in your area**. Watch how they work and live. Take notes on how they handle situations and how much business they are doing. The longer you are in real estate the more you will understand the attitude and lifestyle you should be shooting for. The top producers do the same things over and over. They have figured out what works and what doesn't work, removing what doesn't work from their life. Like a sculptor chipping away at marble to reveal the exquisite statue within, masters at any trade discard the worthless pieces, keeping the parts that work.

Top producing realtors have kept what works, and then they simply do those things repeatedly. They work the same hours every day. They handle all situations the same way. They always display the same demeanor. They do these things so consistently for so long that they eventually become known for them. When you create a widespread belief that you have certain habits or characteristics, these habits become your *reputation*.

Your **reputation** is something you must groom every day. The way people view your character is the foundation of your business, because your business is a "people business." Who you are in the eyes of others will determine if a new client decides to do business with you... or not. You should start building a strong reputation today, right this second. Start doing the things that will build great respect from others, and do those things the same way every time. Reputation not only follows us everywhere, it precedes us; your reputation enters a room before you do! Obviously, if you build a great reputation, great things will happen to you. If you build a bad reputation, you will not be afforded the same opportunities.

There are four areas that you must focus on to build a solid reputation. Focus on these four areas even when no one is looking. Remember, fake it 'til you make it, but once you make it, you can't fake it any longer. People must come to know the real you. Authentic. Genuine. This must be your lifestyle, your identity.

The first area to focus on is hard work. Build a reputation of being the hardest working agent in your office. It all starts at home when you wake up in the morning. Get up early and get to work. Try to be the first one to the office every day. When the other agents start to see your car parked in the same spot consistently for months and months, they will start to realize that you are the hardest working agent there. Your clients will notice as well. People will start talking about seeing your car at the office early and late every single day. This will create a positive buzz about you around town. Stay all day, only leaving for appointments and lunch, and then leave at the same time each day. This is a great way to start building your reputation as the hardest working, most-consistent agent around.

Of course, if you merely show up so people see your car every day, but you aren't *working*, that's a problem. You must take advantage of every second at the office with actions that make you the most money.

Again, find the hardest working, highest producing agent in your office, and study his or her business. How many sales do they close each month and each year? How many listings do they have and how many do they get each month? What type of property do they focus on? How many mail-outs and phone calls do they make? How many hours do they work? How do they handle certain situations? What is their overall demeanor? How do they dress? Etc. As you start finding the answers to these questions, you will slowly develop a pattern for success.

If you work for a very small company or just don't have any high producing agents in your office, reach out to the entire market and find a local agent who is producing at a high volume. Find a top producer, figure out how hard they work, and *out-work them*. Make it a competition in your mind. Work more hours, make more calls, send more emails/mail-outs, contact more people, set up more appointments, and show more property.

If you do this day in and day out, you will soon be getting more listings, writing more contracts and closing more deals than the top producer you studied. You will then become the highest producing agent in your market. You will have the reputation of being the hardest working agent who produces the most sales. People will be drawn to you because they know you work hard and get results.

This high level of success does not happen overnight. It may take years. But when you get there, you will feel great. Nothing makes a person feel better than working hard for something and achieving one's goals. Let people know you work hard *by* working hard, even when no one is looking.

The second area to focus on is *honesty*. Build a strong reputation of being extremely honest, at all times and in all ways, no matter what. If someone asks you a question and you do not know the answer, don't pretend you have an answer. Tell them you do not know. Go find the correct answer and bring it back to them, or direct them to the right person to best answer their question.✶When you handle this situation the correct way, every single time, you become known as the agent who may not know everything, but will always dig up the correct answers.

✶Never fear questions that you can't answer. You will often be asked about things outside your expertise, regardless of how long you have been in business or how educated you are. So get used to it. Just go find the correct answers and get back to them. Quickly.

This will build your reputation of honesty, because people will appreciate that you didn't just toss out an answer that you *thought* might be right. Agents who don't know an answer but try to fake it based on an assumption or guess will have an odor about them; it is called B.S., which is exactly why that term is named after something smelly in a cow pasture.

Even if you are well-meaning but try to invent an answer because you fear looking unintelligent, sooner or later you will get caught giving an untrue answer and lose credibility with your client. Once that happens, the deal is dead. There is almost a zero chance to recover your client's trust.✶The most unintelligent thing to do is to give a false answer. It's better to say you don't know.

No agent in the entire world knows every answer to every question. With all the different properties in the world, there is no way for anyone to know every detail. Your job is not to answer the questions, it's to **get their list of questions and go find the answers.**

* Maintain your integrity. And revel in the high level of honesty that you operate under. This will take you far in life and business.

* A related aspect of integrity is to always **do what you say you are going to do when you say you are going to do it.** It's called being dependable. Show up to every meeting and appointment on time. Send every email when you said you would send it. When people know they can depend on you, that you are always honest and that you are known as a hard worker, you have 90% of your competition beat. And remember, you will sleep much better at night when you know you have treated everyone you meet honestly and professionally. Otherwise, you'll stay up all night worrying and become less productive during the day. Do the right thing and watch your business flourish.

* **The third area to focus on** to build a great reputation is to **be easy to get along with**. This is another important building block for your career. It's the little things that matter in this business and if you can get the little things down, the rest is even smaller potatoes. Always be the agent who is easy to get along with, easy to work with. This means that when something gets under your skin and upsets you, take a deep breath and let it slide off your back like water on a duck.

Everything will not happen the way you envisioned it from the beginning. Sometimes it's someone's fault and sometimes it's nobody's fault. Either way, you must maintain complete composure and not show your negative emotions. Showing your emotions when you are upset will do nothing positive for you or your career. Become known as the agent who always has a positive outlook regardless of the situation. This will draw people to you and draw other agents in your area to want to do business with you.

If a deal falls through, do not become upset about it. Tell everyone involved that you hate it couldn't work out, and move on. It's called being professional. Do everything you can to keep it together, even knowing that some deals just will not close. You can't worry about the ones that get away. If you plan to grow your business to a multi-million dollar level, you will have plenty of deals fall through. It is part of it. Where one door closes, another one opens.

If a deal falls through and it was your listing, this is your opportunity to be professional and show your seller how great of an agent you are by handling the situation smoothly and letting them know that these things happen and that you will resell the property soon enough. Maintain the relationship with a positive, kind attitude even in the worst of situations. Thus they will learn to trust you to handle other tough situations the same way, and your relationship grows.

If the deal falls through and it was your buyer, do what you can to correct the reason the deal fell through and/or find them another property. Keep pushing forward with the greatest of attitudes the entire time. Having a positive attitude will bring great things your way and will also rub off on others. Hey, in the whole scheme of things, we are all only on God's green earth for a short period of time anyway. Enjoy being alive and empower others with a massively positive attitude.

When dealing with other agents in your market, go above and beyond to be easy to work with. Agents in your market are your team, your allies out there on the front lines alongside you trying to sell your listings. You need very strong relationships with the other agents in your market and they need to know that they can depend on you to handle dicey situations in a positive manner. You want to be known as the agent that everyone loves to work with.

✦This is so vital, it deserves repeating: be respectful always and never get upset. If there is an agent who gets under your skin, just smile and take care of business. You cannot get around working with this agent, and you probably can't control their personality. But **you can control your response.** Being in the same market, you will run into them on a deal from time to time. Do not allow the personal problems you may have with another agent to get in the way of business. Be pleasant, have good manners and treat everyone with respect always—and watch your reputation rise to another level.

✦The **fourth and last area to focus on** when building a great reputation is to **always have a low-pressure approach with everyone**. I built my entire career upon this. All my clients know that I will never pressure them into anything that they don't want to do. Therefore, they feel comfortable with me. They also know they can always come to me and talk about anything that might be on their mind, and I won't pressure them. For example, if an owner is just curious of what their property is worth, but they absolutely are not ready to sell just yet, they know they can come to me and talk about the market and what their property might be worth without me trying to pressure them into listing it. If they feel trust and comfort with you, they will always come back to you when they do decide it's time to pull the trigger and list their property.

If I am showing property to a buyer, and I get the feeling (or if they straight up tell me) they aren't going to buy anything today, that's fine with me. I do not want anyone to do something that they are not 100% certain they want to do. It is my job from day one to prequalify each buyer before we start looking at properties and make sure what their intentions are. And, at the end of the day when the deal closes, my goal is that everyone involved is happy with the deal because it was their decision in the first place.

*My job is not to pressure clients into doing deals. My job is to provide the most information I can so that they decide how and when to proceed. From there, I do the other part of my job, which is constant follow-up to help them accomplish their goals.*If they decide not to pull the trigger today, this is a great opportunity to build the relationship and have that in place for the day that they do want to proceed with a deal. When the time arrives, what agent are they going to come back to? An agent who tried to pressure them into an unwanted deal and who made them feel extremely uncomfortable? Or the agent who put them at ease, having their best interests in mind?*Chances are very high that they will come back to you, the agent they felt most comfortable with.*They will also refer their friends and family to you.*The low-pressure approach gives you a great opportunity to do business and get lots of referrals.

Sure, some car salesmen achieve sales using high-pressure tactics… but they rarely stay in the same location for long. They fail to get repeat customers. Most buyers have become sophisticated. They resent high-pressure salesmen. They know they can walk away and find another car lot that will treat them better—or another realtor.*Have a low-pressure lifestyle. Remember to handle all situations the same way. Show consistency to your clients and they will always come back to you.

I am telling you how to build a huge business with a great reputation. Spending your energy on these four areas is crucial to a high level of success. One false move could hurt your reputation and could cost you a long string of clients and referrals. However, we all make mistakes. None of us are perfect. When you make a mistake, own up to it and move on. This will clear your conscience as well as creating a chance to patch things up. Learn from your mistakes and keep pressing forward, remembering that a solid reputation can survive the inevitable, occasional oops.

Let's further consider the value of a great reputation: it creates a **multiplication effect**. When you treat one client well, they eventually tell a friend about you. They tell their friend how hardworking, honest, easy to work with and low-pressure you were. Now BOOM! That friend thinks, "Wow, Ricky sounds like an outstanding agent. I will definitely call him when *I* decide to buy or sell."

And just like that, you have now created a relationship with your past client's friend without even being there or meeting the person. So, that person sees your signs and advertisements around town, and one day they decide to buy a house. Who do they call? That's right. They call you up, remembering their friend's good words about you now that they are ready to buy. Over the next year, your original client might be asked by five people, "Do you know a good realtor?" That's a multiplication of five. Beautiful. Even more beautiful is when you stay in this business long enough that those 5 clients each multiplied again to 25. I don't have to tell you that multiplication is much better than addition!

This is a great example of what a strong reputation will do for you. It's almost like cloning yourself several times and sending a team of yourselves out there in the market to bring in future business. For me, it's like have a big team of imaginary Ricky's running around spreading the word about how great of a job I do for my clients. It all stems from doing the little things the same way every single day long enough to become known for it—developing the lifestyle and reputation of a top producer. How bad do you want it? Hopefully bad enough to do what it takes. Start doing the little things it takes to build a great reputation today, then watch your business grow and grow.

3: The Importance of Time

Time is the greatest tool we have. It can work for you or against you. The agents who do not use it to their advantage don't even realize how much it works against them. They get caught up with something trivial and before they know it, the day is over. We've all heard, "Time is money." Sure. But it is more complex than... and in fact, time is *more* valuable than money. You can always make more money. But can you create more time? Only God can do that! Be grateful of the time God gives you. Treasure every second. Know that time is going to pass you by regardless of how you spend it. So spend it as wisely as you can.

In real estate, time goes by super-fast. You should be careful of what you spend it on. The truth is, just about everyone has the social skills it takes to be successful in real estate. That's not the problem. What holds back most agents is not knowing how to spend their time and being unaware of what steals too many valuable minutes. The ability to manage your time in a way that maximizes your results and reduces wasted time is a key skill. The more experience you gain, the better you will get at spotting situations that are not worth your time.

Often I see agents in the market who have all the skills necessary to get out there and be great agents. However, they jam up their time with clients and activities that don't payoff. I'm not the first person to write about time management, but again, it is more complex than just using a "to-do" list or fancy Calendar/Planner. It starts with psychology and attitude. Most of us approach life one event at a time, with a laid back attitude of "I'll eventually get all these things done." That's a psychology rooted in the illusion that time is unlimited. That's what psychologist's call "magical thinking," meaning *the opposite of reality.* No, you *won't* get everything done that needs to be done.

Stop thinking that way! Instead, adopt a psychology of ✶**maximizing your time per transaction**.

A newer agent asked me for advice on a deal they were working on. Of course, I was happy to help. They told me the situation and asked what I would do if I were in their shoes. The situation was that they were working with a buyer who was very motivated to buy a house. However, after trying to get the client pre-approved for a loan, they found out that their credit score was not good enough to buy a house right away. The lender told the buyer how to improve their credit score—steps that would take several months to process. Only after the score came up would they be able to buy a house. After hearing the situation, I asked the agent, "So, what do you need help with?" The reply: "What can I do at this point to make the deal work?"

By then, it was clear to me that this particular deal was all the agent had thought about all day. I continued: "Well, let me ask you, what other deals are you working on today?" The agent confessed, "Nothing else right now. I am just trying to figure out a way to make this one work." Once they said that, I knew exactly what I was dealing with: an agent who did not realize that time was working against them even as we stood there talking. It was not a problem with the deal. This was a problem with the agent not being mindful of time and using it to their advantage. I assured the agent that they had done a fantastic job with that buyer and that there was nothing else they could do until the buyer completes the steps to increase their credit score. Then I had a heart to heart with them. I told them that wasting the entire day on how we can magically get a buyer's credit score up is not the way to become a successful agent.

The way to handle this situation—and every situation —is to push it to the farthest point you can, keeping good notes on it and (later) checking on it from time to time, but immediately move on to other deals. There was nothing else the agent could do with that deal; they had done all they could. I encouraged the agent to follow up with the buyer once a week or so until they can purchase the house. Then, represent them on the purchase. There you have it: You made the deal work. Nothing else to worry about. All the agent could do at that point was move on, and later spend 5-10 minutes a week following up with the buyer, making sure they are working on their credit.*Meanwhile, stack up other deals in their pipeline until that one comes through (if it comes through at all).

You see my point. This agent was wasting hours on *one* deal, thinking and contemplating, when all they needed was 5 minutes a week set aside for this one while continuing to find other possible deals. As soon as the agent heard me say this, it was like a light bulb went off in their head. *Maximize time per transaction by moving to the next transaction as soon as one stalls.* I could tell that what I said had resonated.

I see other agents doing similar things with all kinds of situations. They waste more time than they need to on negotiations, inspections, tweaking their websites, carefully crafting letters, etc. Don't spend all your time working on one or two deals. Spend less time on current deals and more time on procuring new deals by making phone calls, sending emails, letters, postcards, having open houses, etc. These are the activities that make you money... not diddling with your website, making fancier business cards, calling friends to gossip, chit-chatting with agents in the office, or worrying about if a deal is going to work out. Yes, do have a website, do have business cards, and of course ensure that your current deals are moving forward. But do these types of activities *after* you have completed your money-making activities of the day. *Pay close attention to what makes you money and what doesn't.

Then, use this knowledge and experience to help yourself make decisions that best suit your time and worth.

Where do I start in prioritizing actions for making money? **Talking**. Not with the pointless "chit-chatting" I just mentioned, but talking with potential clients/listings. **If you are talking with people, you are making money!** That is, if the people you are talking with are clients, future clients, or in conversations that will lead directly to other future clients/listings. And when I say "talking with," the emphasis is on *with*: that means during conversations, spend 80% of the time *listening* to them and only 20% actually speaking yourself. Talk less and listen more. That's a specific example of a dollar-productive activity; now let's return to the broad approach to maximizing time.

When it comes to the subject of what you should do with your time that will be most productive, you must **think big**. Huge. Look at the big picture. One deal is not the "make it or break it" of your career. No single deal will make the difference in your great success as an agent. If it is to be that you become a top producer, with hundreds and even thousands of deals under your belt one day, you must think bigger than one deal. Yes, take care of your deals and go above and beyond to secure a deal and the relationship therein. However, this is not the goal.

The goal is to create a business that produces *hundreds* of deals. How do you do this? It's simple. Spend most of your time working on the big picture and little time on current deals. Avoid getting caught up in the same cycle of business that most agents end up in, where they spend all their time working on current deals and no time working on an abundance of future deals. Most of the time, working on an abundance of future deals will bring you plenty of current business as well. So it is a win/win.

What activities create a huge quantity of future deals while giving us enough deals in the present? Answer: *Projects*. You should always be involved in a project aimed at securing more business. And as you complete each project, already be preparing to move immediately to the next one. Your career will then be made up of a series of different, completed projects that produce a massive amount of business—providing plenty of deals for the present while securing your future. In other words, by focusing on your future results, you will *accidently* run into deals for the present. It is called karma. If you are doing the things that you know you are supposed to be doing, good things will happen. The things you are supposed to be doing include working hard every day (all day) to contact large amounts of property owners, being honest, dependable and a help to others. If you take these actions consistently, you will prosper now and in the future.

Here are some examples of projects:

- Calling all FSBO's in your area

- Sending a group of owners a mailing

- Sending a mass email

- Calling all Expired/Withdrawn Listings

- Cold calling a subdivision/complex

- Calling past clients

- Following-up on all past leads

- Contacting your Sphere of Influence

- Finding a buyer for one of your listings

- Finding a listing for one of your (or another agent's) buyers.

These are just a few examples of different projects you could undertake. Your job is to come up with project after project.

It is not hard to come up with projects. Put yourself in contact with hundreds of owners. Do not ponder long about what project to do. This is wasting valuable time. Pick one and go. Then pick another and go.

Look in your MLS at the properties that have recently closed and been put under contract/pending. Looking through this list will give you ideas of different projects you can begin. *For example, if you see that a property in a particular area has sold or been placed under contract, you can contact the surrounding owners and let them know about the recent activity. Possibilities are endless; there is always new market info to share. *Be an information provider*. Keep everyone informed of the recent market info at all times. This will prove to everyone that you are a market specialist.

Multi-Tasking and Time-Multiplying: *Top producers both multiply their time and multi-task. These are similar yet distinct methods of time management. The quickest/simplest way to multiply your efforts is to delegate. We will examine that topic in a later chapter, including the idea of hiring an assistant. For now, even if you cannot afford an assistant or secretary or whatever, with a bit of creativity, you may be able to think of ways to get other people to do some of your more basic tasks, thus multiplying your time. That may be as simple as having a family member help out, or using an outside service for various tasks. Within your own real estate office, there are likely people who are eager to help you with projects and tasks. We will return to this topic later.

Even without a staff, you can immediately begin to **multi-task**. Some people can do this much better than others.

A few people have a brain wired for "true," full multitasking: actually able to do three things at once. Some cannot do that at all, or fool themselves into thinking they are multi-tasking when really they are merely switching their brain back and forth between tasks and not really saving time. You must pay attention to how well you multitask, and work on it if you can.

For many people, the best way to multi-task is to first identify which task requires the most concentration and brainpower. Then identify a second task that is rather mindless, usually something that requires more physical work than mental work. Focus on the first mental task while also doing the menial task mindlessly. But the main point of multi-tasking, in real estate, is to avoid wasting time waiting for a result from one project before beginning another. Always keep several fires burning at once.

When you see a top producer with ten to twenty pending contracts and fifty or more active listings, and they just act like nothing is going on, he or she are great multi-taskers. They can handle many things at once mentally and physically. Once they get a listing or negotiate a contract, they somewhat forget about it and move on to the next one. After a while, listings and contracts pile up. You may think that would keep them busy, but it doesn't. They find more.

While all of those deals are happening, top producers still have time to seek more listings, contracts and projects. Why? Because, once they do a deal or get a listing, they forget about it and only check on it from time to time to make sure all is well. This allows them to focus on finding more business. That is what got them there in the first place: multiple projects. They spend very little time checking on their listings and contracts, allowing the natural process to do its own work, while moving on to their next project.

One More *Time*: Learning comes by repetition… so let me emphasize again the point of this chapter: *most agents underestimate the value of time.** Time slips right though their fingers like water. The difference in an agent who makes $75,000 and one who makes $250,000 is literally as slim a margin as an Olympian who loses a race by .02 seconds. It is so close it boggles my mind. It all boils down to how well the agent preserves and uses time. *Unsuccessful realtors allow time to flow by passively. Top producers actively multi-task and multiply themselves and their time, and they don't take time management for granted. Take time seriously. It is the most important yet hidden part of success in real estate or any business. *Multiply your time and multiply your life!

Section II:

The Actions of a Top Producing Real Estate Agent

4: What Makes You Money

Specifically, beyond the general ideas already mentioned, what is the Number One activity that makes you money as an agent? Closings. I can guarantee that nothing you do makes you more money as a real estate agent than having closings. Do you agree? As stated in the first chapter, closings are the most consistent things that happen in the universe. Maybe that's an overstatement... but if you watch local and national MLS listings, year after year there is not a single day without a closing. Even in the worst of years for real estate, there are still closings every day.

It makes me laugh when I hear people say that real estate is not consistent. They just don't realize how consistent real estate is. Real estate has no more ups and downs than any other business. Take Walmart, for example. Some days Walmart sells more than on other days, but no one would say Walmart is "inconsistent." The Walton family is consistently making tons of money, regardless of daily "ups and downs" in gross sales.

In the realty business, we face tough competition and a steep learning curve, so it's not easy to get started. But it is still, *consistently*, a profitable business. People assume it's not consistent because most realtors don't succeed and must go back to the so-called "regular paycheck." The only thing consistent about most folks' paychecks is that they never increase beyond meager cost-of-living raises. A consistently-bad paycheck is still a bad paycheck! Real estate can be, and *should* be, more profitable and more consistent than a 9-to-5 job.

Most jobs are not truly "consistent": you can get fired or laid off from a regular job at any time. In some businesses, employee turnover is over 50% per year! Is that consistent? In real estate, you are your own boss. You make all the executive decisions. Are you going to fire yourself? No. Are you going to give yourself a fat pay raise? You can!

If you add *action* to the principals in this book, you will have consistent closings throughout the ups and downs of any market. That will result in a fat pay raise. That is freedom. This business provides an opportunity to be free of the "consistent" salary limit found in most jobs.

So how do we break through the stereotype and claim our share of the closings that are happening each day? The answer is easier than most people realize. Real estate is fun when you have consistent closings. Once you reach that point in your career, your life gets noticeably better and easier. To find the secret to having consistent closings, let's look at the step-by-step process of a closing.

From Finding Prospects to Closing: The Process

First, you must find a potential prospect and have an initial conversation with them about their real estate needs and goals. Second, you must follow up with them through an appointment or phone call. Then, when they are ready, you must convert that prospect into a client though a listing or purchase agreement. After that, you negotiate the deal, and finally process and close the transaction. Got it? Let's list the steps:

1. **Find Prospects**
2. **Follow Up via Call/Appointment/Relationship**
3. **Conversion (Client Contract)**
4. **Negotiate a Deal**
5. **Process and Close the Deal**

All real estate transactions in the history of mankind have been created and closed via this same process. It is the not-so-secret formula that leads to every closing. Now, how do we insert ourselves successfully into as many of these equations as possible? Well, per the formula, begin with the first step: Finding a prospect. This is both the first and the *most important* part of the equation. Without this step, the process stops right then and there. Thus, as a realtor, this must be your most important priority every day.

How do I find more prospects? Every agent has a different way of finding new prospects. There are hundreds of different ways to do this. The trick is to pick what works for you. I suggest trying methods that are working for others until you find success. Success in finding prospects consists of two things: *making sure you are finding the best **quality prospects**, and that you are finding **enough quantity of prospects**.* This is another sentence you should write down, post and review from time to time. And take note that quality comes before quantity.

Most agents get stuck in low production mode because they start finding prospects and think they are on the right track. They settle. They forget that there are different levels of quality when it comes to prospects. As I've mentioned, we want the highest quality prospects we can find. This saves us time and allows us to make much more money. Be wary of low-quality prospects. They will eat your career away before you even know it by burning up too much of your time.

Using the method that enables you to find the right number of prospects is also key to achieving a high sales goal. This is where [*thinking big*] comes into play. Make sure you are working on prospecting projects that will yield hundreds, even thousands, of prospects over the long haul—while targeting the highest-quality prospects.

Of the many ways to find prospects, it makes sense for me to share with you the tools I use myself—tools I've proven can help you become the highest producer in your market. Of course, I get business from all kinds of sources/tools. Random deals come along through referrals, sign calls, friends, repeat business, and even sheer luck. However, I don't focus on any other method of finding prospects except for what I'm about to share. You may have heard this before, but I am telling you from firsthand experience that this is the most effective way to find the highest quality prospects within any market.

Discover and Claim Your Place in the Market

First, you must decide your niche in the market. Some agents sell primary homes. Others sell commercial properties, while others sell vacation/second homes. There are even agents who only sell properties in a particular subdivision or condominium complex. Whatever your niche is to be, *you* must decide. You can't be a master of all niches though—that is for certain.

My niche is beachfront condos on the Gulf of Mexico, but that doesn't mean I haven't sold residential apartment complexes and single-family homes. If a deal comes your way and it makes financial sense to spend time on it, absolutely take it even if the property doesn't fit the exact criteria of your niche. The point is to *concentrate* on a type of property that you feel will bring you the best return; focus on an area in which you will enjoy being a specialist.

Ideally, your place in the market will not be oversaturated; it will be an area or type of real estate that has room for you. But don't be afraid of competition. It is unlikely that you will find any niche where someone else has not already "staked a claim." Competition is everywhere; it is unavoidable. Steve Jobs did not invent the computer and cell phone industries.

Many others were making and selling computers and phones long before he did. But Jobs did not give up and say, "Others beat me to it, so I won't make Macs and iPhones." He just worked harder and smarter and with more creativity. And now Apple is the richest corporation on earth.

How do you find your niche? Look around. I suggest talking to other agents and researching supply and demand of different properties in your market.✶Look for properties that have a good average sales price and frequent turnover. Research online, use word-of-mouth, do in-person "tours": driving around your region with open eyes and an open mind. Pick out your niche and start communicating with buyers and sellers in that market immediately. Today!

For example, if you decide you want to start selling houses in a subdivision, *after researching that market* (all recent listings and sales), the next step is to start communicating with the owners in that subdivision. Send them letters and postcards. Call them. Make contact. The sooner you make contact, the sooner your relationship will begin and the quicker you will make deals happen. Follow up with the ones with whom you had a good connection. Become their friend. Over time, these friendships will turn into closings and referrals.

Run ads in your local paper and real estate magazines/booklets, seeking buyers of the type of property you picked. The point is to select what type of property you want to sell and start contacting people right now. Don't waste any time. Later, we will discuss in more detail what to say to these owners when you call them. But for now I just want you to accept the key principle: select your niche and immediately start making contacts!

✶ First, we want to discover all we can before we make contact. When did they buy the property? How much did they pay? Is there a mortgage? Do they live there or is it an investment or second home? *Et cetera.*

Then as you eventually talk to them, take good notes on how the conversation went and what was talked about. The goal is to talk to as many of the owners you can, just to find out if there is a connection between you and them, if there is anything you can do for them right now and if it is okay to stay in touch via email about the market.

Many agents make contact and try to push the prospect to do a deal on the first call. This is not my strategy. I want to have a conversation to find out if I connect with the prospect. If I do, then a relationship has begun and I will stay in close contact with them forever. If not, then *no harm, no foul.* I will still send them postcards and letters. You never know if they will come back around to you later. However, I will mostly focus on the ones with whom I had a good connection and an enjoyable conversation.

When you add a new "farm group" of owners to your database, the plan is long-term. You will send this group mail-outs every six weeks… forever. Consistency is the key to everything, even mail-outs. Since every group of owners that I add to my master list will be in the same niche market, I can send them all the same mail-outs.

Occasionally, I will send a special mail-out designed specifically for certain groups, but most of the time I send the same postcard or letter to all of them. It's more time-efficient. As a side note, every time I list or sell a property I do send a postcard out to the other owners in the same area whether they are in my farm group or not.

Once you pick your niche within your market that you want to focus on and become a specialist, it's time to get to work. Immediately start designing a mailing, beginning with 50-100 addresses. At the same time, begin making phone calls. After you've exhausted calling every phone number you can find, it's time to add more to the list.

Little by little, you grow this database of owners, mailing to as many as you can afford every six weeks, until you get to the number of people that you feel will eventually push you to the top. This number will be in the several thousands, but start small and build your way up slowly. Only add more owners after you have called every single phone number you can find of the last group you added.

*This process will take years. But in the process, slowly but surely you will build the foundation of a huge business that will never be fazed by market downturns. You will have such a great base of relationships with property owners that nothing will bring you down. The big difference in this and other methods is that by following up the mail-outs with phone calls, you *talk* to your future clients to make a connection from the beginning, which is far more effective than just sending mail and *wondering* if you might connect.

Phone Calls: Absolutely Positively Essential

By calling these owners instead of waiting on them to call you (which rarely happens!), you will find that some owners are ready to buy or sell right away. This gives you an opportunity to represent them as their real estate agent immediately*If you are not making calls along with your mail-outs, you are missing out on tons of business.

*This is where consistent closings, repeat business and loads of referrals live. Hey, if it's worth building, it's worth building right! Most agents will not make the calls, and therefore will not do the business. They think that sending mail is enough. If you are sending mail without a follow-up phone call, chances are just about as good of you finding business if you never sent the mail in the first place. Seriously! Without the calls, you are toast.

Here's another secret: most people don't like to make phone calls. We could examine the various psychological reasons behind that, but it's a waste of time to diagnose the problem because I already have the cure: **Just do it!** If it were easy, everyone would do it. It's not easy, but making the effort to make regular phone calls is worth it. Make the sacrifice and get to work, and don't waste time with rationalizations, fooling yourself into thinking, "It's easier and faster just to send emails and postcards."

Now that you know the most effective way to find the highest quality prospects in your market, it's time to capitalize on this breakthrough. One important fact I want you to know is that this method produces an unlimited number of prospects. These are the highest quality prospects produced at an unlimited rate. Trust me, there is no way anyone could possibly contact every single property owner in the market. Therefore, new prospects are always out there for you. So capitalize on this.

Okay, you are committed for the long-term, you have chosen your niche, you have completed your mail-outs, you called every single owner you could find and took notes on all those conversations. You made great connections. Some owners you talked with indicated that they may be interested in buying or selling soon. Now what? This is your opportunity to ask for an appointment to meet and discuss the situation further. Or, if they are not local, call them and talk in depth about their plans and email them the specific information they need in order to make a decision. If they are looking to buy, email them a list of properties that fit their criteria. If they are thinking of selling, ask to see the property so that you can make a fair assessment of what the property might sell for, and consider if the property might interest your buying clients.

Follow up and take these situations as far as you can until they either tell you they are ready to move forward or not.

If not, back off but stay in touch. Remember: stay low-pressure. Develop relationships using these opportunities to demonstrate your professionalism. If you treat them well when they are merely inquiring, they will come back to you when they decide to take the next step.

Follow each prospect down the path of their choice. If you are contacting the number of prospects that you should be, and do as I am telling you here, you will start to have plenty of activity—and transactions will follow. Fill up your pipeline of relationships with property owners and you won't have to worry about one or two deals.

Once the prospect decides to pull the trigger to either put their property on the market or make an offer on a property, it's time to convert them into a client via a written contract. At some point, the prospect either tells you they are ready or gives you signals that they are ready. Sometimes, when you see the correct signals, you must ask for the business before they will admit that they are ready. These signals are different for everyone. Becoming good at catching the signals of a prospect ready to pull the trigger comes from repeated experience with buyers and sellers. So, get out in the market and start gaining experience.

While prospecting and meeting with buyers and sellers, watch for the trigger signals and be ready to ask for the business at the right time. The two questions I use are simple: "Are you ready to put it on the market?" or "Are you ready to make an offer?"

Again, do not force it. Wait for the right opportunity. The longevity of the relationship and the years of business and referrals are far more important than trying to force a quick deal. Be mindful of this. The reason this system of talking to property owners and staying low pressure works so well is that these people are the heart of the market, in unlimited numbers. You are aiming at the heart of the market, contacting as many as you can. This enables you to create as much business as you can handle at any given time.

* If you become overwhelmed with business, you can cut back on prospecting. Later, if things begin to slow down and you need more business, just pick up the phone and start creating more business until you are loaded up again. This system keeps you busy while putting you in the best position possible with the people in the market who matter most to your success.

Buyers vs. Sellers

Let's talk about pursuing listings (sellers) versus buyers.
* You must have listings to be highly successful. Listings are an agent's lifeline. Look at the top producers in the country.
* These agents are primarily *listing* agents.*For years, my ratio has been 80% sellers and 20% buyers.*And the way this process plays out, buyers will come from your efforts to list property.

It may seem obvious that people who just sold a piece of property will likely be looking to buy soon.*Put more emphasis on marketing to find listings than to find buyers, because the buyers come more naturally. *An owner eventually wants to buy, or a buyer finds your listing and calls you.

If you happen to focus upon being a buyer's agent, that's okay. You might make a good living.*However, only the agents who have a large inventory of well-priced listings will be at the top of the food chain in any given market.
* With a large inventory of good listings, you can go find more listings while other realtors (buyer's agents) show and sell your current listings.*This gives you an opportunity to multiply your time among a plethora of properties instead of spending most of your time working on just one or two.

I work with buyers all the time, but I pick and choose the ones I want to work with. I always work with referrals and repeat clients regardless of the situation for the sake of maintaining relationships. Relationships trump everything. So, at the end of the day, focus on obtaining listings and take what buyers come from those efforts. This is your most effective strategy.

I love the opportunity to help an owner buy another property. When I work with a current owner that is planning to purchase, this gives me a great opportunity to show them how professional I am through the process of helping someone *buy* a property. This in turn instills confidence in them about my abilities to be their listing agent when the time comes for them to sell. This way I am planting seeds for multiple deals with the same client.

At the end of the day, it's a numbers game. You *will* connect successfully with a percentage of people you contact, regardless of your skill level. The agent that contacts the most prospects wins. So get to work!

5: What to Say

Prospects are easy to find. They are everywhere you look. If you want to sell commercial property, look at all the businesses and commercial properties in your area while you drive around. If it's single-family homes, look how many subdivisions there are where you live. The possibilities are endless.

Once you realize that closings happen every single day and prospects are everywhere, you now have faith that being successful in real estate might be a little easier than you thought. You start going through the steps of the closing formula. You start finding prospects and making calls. But what do you say and how do you talk to prospects? Don't worry, that is what I am here for—to help you through this process and get you to a place in your career where you can enjoy a consistent income.

Before I get into what you should say to prospects when you call them, I want to throw a few facts out as food for thought. A study recently showed that 90% of the real estate business generated in today's market is generated the old-fashioned way, through mail-outs and phone calls. Now think about that for a minute. Almost all business generated in today's great world of technology is generated by "snail mail" and personal phone calls. All the other types of real estate business *combined* only generate the other 10%.

This should be a breakthrough moment for you. You now know where a 90% market share of business comes from. Social media, websites and other tech-based marketing methods have their place, but now you know how small that "place" is, in relative terms. So where would you pour most of your efforts if you have the choice? Into the 90%, right?

Look, I am telling you where the business is. All you have to do is take action. It is right there in front of your nose. With 90% of the results, it would be okay if mail-outs and phone calls were all you focused on! I personally spend very little time on social media and technology. And I don't pay for any **leads**. Leads you pay for are not the quality leads you want. So let's look deeper into the 90% mail-outs and phone calls.

When you send mailings, on average your success rate will be around **3%** over the long term (3-5 years). Not bad, but not that great either. So success depends on how many mail-outs you are sending and what you are putting on your mail-outs. Also, It takes an average of seven pieces of mail before a prospect really gets your name stuck in their head. However, if you add a simple phone call into the mix, your success rate jumps from 3% to a whopping **18%**.

That is astonishing! A call makes all the difference. It could be as simple as a call to ask if they have been receiving your mail and if there is anything you can do for them. With that simple (and free) act, you've increased your success rate by **600%**! Bells should be going off in your head right now. This business is already tough enough. If there is a way that you can up your chances of success by 600% for free, there is no way that you should allow that opportunity to pass you by.

Now you know where 90% of the business is and how to increase your chances of success in that area by 600%. This business is much easier than most agents make it. The trick is that it is mostly mental. Understanding how business is created, setting your mind to the Nike slogan (Just do it!), and having the ability to duplicate the creation process repeatedly like a machine—these mental efforts separate the high producers from the low.

*For extreme efficiency, the perfect and doable number of calls to make is 20-30 calls each day, 2-3 days a week. You might want to do more in the beginning of you career.

There were several days early in my career when I made 50-100 calls. I had that kind of hunger for success. However, regardless of how experienced or inexperienced you are, 20-30 calls, 2-3 days a week is enough to produce huge results without taking up very much time at all. That still leaves you time on the remaining days for other business tasks. These are the most efficient numbers I have found that work. You should find what works for you and the level you wish to reach. At the minimum, especially in the beginning of your career, if you want to double and triple your income, then make 20-30 calls, 2-3 days a week.

Okay, we know we must make phone calls to survive in this business. Even if our main source of leads come from the internet, without calling them you will not succeed at even a medium level, much less a very high level. Now it's time to target the people you want to call, and find phone numbers.

*The best way to find a person's phone number is online. There are dozens of great websites that will help you locate phone numbers based on limited information. Go to Google, put in **"reverse phone lookup"** and you'll see options. You are not actually using the "reverse phone lookup" feature (that's when a number shows up on your caller ID, and you want to know their name). But the same online companies also provide a simple way to type in a name OR an address to find the likely phone number associated with it. Some of these sites are free and some charge a fee. The offers and terms change, which is why I suggest you Google it for yourself. If you don't know the name of the owner of a particular piece of property, go to the county tax records. These are also found easily online at the official government website for your county.

You enter the address and *sometimes* the current owner's name is shown. Some counties may also show a phone number, but in most cases, you would then take their name back to the reverse phone number site. Knowing both the name and the address increases the chance of finding correct phone numbers. Also, ask your broker what systems and websites your company uses to find owner information.

Search high and low. If you can find a directory of a group of people, it is extremely helpful: civic club memberships, church directories (most churches only give these to their members), Chamber of Commerce directories, social groups, etc. Find the numbers and get ready to call... and connect.

Okay, it's time to make your calls. You have blocked out a few hours and everything else is on the back burner. It's good to turn your emails and any other distractions off during this time. Your laser-like focus, your sole purpose, is to get through these 20-30 calls without a single distraction. Now it's time for your pre-call ritual. This is where you take a minute or two to think about what you are doing and what you should be aiming to say during your calls. During this time, you want to breathe (deep breaths!) and relax. You do not want to be nervous once you start making calls. The person on the other end of the phone can hear if you are nervous by the tone of your voice. It is hard to hide it. At the same time, you don't have to have "stage fright," because they aren't seeing your face or judging you with the critical eye a stage performer must face. But if you talk too fast or have a high-pitched voice, you will have a hard time connecting with anyone on the phone.

While people can't see you, experts say that the way you *look* does affect the way you *sound*. If you were dressed in your bathrobe, you will sound less professional than if you were dressed in professional attire and sitting upright.

People can hear you smiling over the phone! They can hear it in your voice. Try this with a friend. Call them and see if they can point out when you are smiling and when you are not. You can also hear the mood of the person you call. Pay close attention to their tone and play into it accordingly.

The entire philosophy behind making sales calls in real estate is the following: *You are **not** selling anything. You are **not** calling prospects to find out if they want to do business with you today. The only underlying reason for your call is to find out if you even want to do future business with them.* You are not calling to see if they want to buy or sell a property today. You are not even calling to see if they would consider you as their realtor if they ever decide to buy or sell. Sure, you might later ask these types of questions to get a reaction. And you may stumble upon someone who is ready to pull the trigger today. However, your sole purpose is to have a conversation and find out if you connect enough to continue a relationship and maybe do some business down the road.

This should take much of the nervousness of making calls away. This is not a typical sales call. You are not a telemarketer. You are offering them yourself and your service, not a Ronco *Vegematic* or a *ShamWow* cleaner. You are simply checking with people to see if there is anything you can do for them now or in the future, and to initiate or solidify a relationship. You can cheerfully conclude, "Okay, we will stay in touch via email, mail-outs and by phone." And of course, show gratitude for the good conversation.

There are all kinds of **phone call scripts**. I have tried them all. *The less "canned" or "rehearsed" they sound, the better. But there are methods that I have created that are a combination of the many scripts I have tried, mixed with a bit of what I have found that works.

The five most important words you can ever use when making your calls is *"How are you doing today?"* This is my secret weapon and has made me very successful. When the prospect answers the phone, I will start, "Mr. Smith? Hey Mr. Smith. This is Ricky Carruth with RE/MAX. How are you doing today?" I say this very clearly. I even slow it down so that they hear my name and the company I am with. Sometimes I don't say it as clear as they need, and they ask, "Who is this?" This is when I tell them I am sorry and then I repeat the entire line a second time just a little slower and pause.

After the initial pleasantries, I am going to go with the flow from there, but what I usually like to do is to start talking about the weather. Yes, the *weather*. I have found that everyone can relate to the weather and it gives me some common ground to start a conversation. If it is a real nice day, I will say something like, "Great! I am doing well, too. Just enjoying this good weather today. Isn't it gorgeous outside?" If it's a rainy day, I will say something like, "Just trying to stay dry over here. It's nasty out there!" Or, I might even ask them, "Are you staying dry today?" Believe it or not, most of the time the prospect will engage in a short conversation with you about the weather. I like this approach and it works well for me to break the tension of a sales call. It's non-threatening. People always want to know about the weather. They want to know what it's doing, what it did and what it's going to do. This is an incredible icebreaker and should be used on every call you make.

Once you get to the end of the weather part of the call, it's time to transition to the **reason** for your call. You don't want to start the transition too early and interrupt them. You also do not want to start too late and allow any awkward pauses. You want the conversation to flow naturally and comfortable.

The only way to get better at this is by making more calls and practicing. I know it's not easy for everyone to get on the phone and make it happen, but just remember: 600%.

The transition to the reason for your call should be smooth and confident. When you reach the end of the weather conversation, which could last 5 seconds or 5 minutes, go right into it. "Mr. Smith, I don't want to take up too much of your time today, but...." I want you to master this transition. You will use this every time, inserting the reason for the call immediately after that phrase.

Your reason should be in the form of a question. Target your prospects with reasons that will interest them. Here are some examples of **reasons to contact prospects:**

- I have been sending you mail for some time, and wanna make sure you're receiving it. Is there anything I can do for you at this time?

- I was calling today to let you know that 3 houses have sold in your subdivision this year, and just wanted to see if there was anything I could do for you?

- I was calling today to let you know that there is a house for sale in your neighborhood and wondered if you or anyone you know may be interested in it?

- I was calling to let you know that a condo in your complex just sold for the highest price in years, so I wanted to reach out to you and see if you are considering selling anytime soon?

- I was calling today to let you know that I have sold 15 houses so far this year in your area, and just wanted to see if there was anything I could do for you today?

- I was calling today to let you know that an agent in my office has a buyer looking for a condo in your complex, so I wanted to see if you guys have considered selling lately?

- I was calling today because your house is for sale by owner. Would you work with me if I brought a buyer? When could I see the house?

- I was calling today because I see that your property expired from the market and would like to know if you are still interested in selling?

These are all good examples of reasons to call. You can come up with hundreds of reasons. Reasons are a dime a dozen. The trick is to come up with a reason that **fits the targeted group of prospects** that you are contacting and run with it. Don't spend any time perfecting the reason to call. Over time, you'll find the ones that work best for you. Remember this: **It doesn't really matter so much what you say, but *how* you say it**. Staying calm and relaxed during the call, but showing energy and passion at the right moments, will give a good impression.

Once you give the reason, it's time to sit back and listen to their reaction. The conversation can go a thousand different directions at this point. By now we have talked to them enough to know if there is any kind of connection or not. Our job at this point is to talk to them further so that we can get to know them as much as we can from your time on the phone. Once the conversation has run its course, it's time to end the call. I call this the relationship-building part of the call. After a great conversation, the time comes to end it. I will say, "Well, thank you for your time today Mr. Smith. Would it be okay if I stayed in touch with you about the market?" This is a great ending to a great call. Depending on their answer, you might ask for additional information, such as a cell phone number and email address.

Another great way to end the call is to make them commit. Commit to what? Commit to using you as their agent in the future. When you make the prospect commit to you verbally that you will be the agent they work with in the future, it creates a bond of their word. My dad told me a long time ago that people are only as good as their word. When they tell you they will use your services when they decide to buy or sell property and you stay in touch with them until that day comes, they really have very little choice in the matter. They already gave you their word, and very few people go back on their word unless you fail to stay in touch. Here is how you do it: When you tell them the reason of your call and they say that they are just not interested, you then say the following, "I understand. Well, one day you will buy or sell a property in the area, and I would like the opportunity to work with you when that day comes. Do you have any agent that you work with?" This statement and question will get to the root of where you stand with this prospect. If they tell you they have a very close friend who is an agent or that they have some really great relationship with another agent, great! That tells you that you might be wasting your time with this person. If they say they do not have an agent or that they had an agent but haven't really talked to them in a long time, perfect. This is your opportunity to ask them the following, "Well, if I stay in touch with you about the market, would you consider me your agent when that day comes?" This will put you in the driver's seat with this client and the green light to stay in touch with them for future deals.

Asking them what day they are available for lunch is also a great way to end the call. Tell them you would like to put a face with the name and get to know them a little more. You are never wasting time by having lunch with a prospect. If you can fill up your lunch calendar everyday with prospects and clients, you will be of better service to them. This face time will help you understand and accomplish their goals.

★ Here is an example of an entire script:

Mr. Smith: -Hello.

Me (Ricky): *-Mr. Smith?*

-Yes, this is Mr. Smith.

-Hey Mr. Smith. This is Ricky Carruth with RE/MAX. How are you doing today?

- We are doing good, Ricky. How about you?

-I am doing great as well...thanks for asking. Just enjoying this beautiful weather we have today. Isn't it gorgeous?

-It sure is, Ricky. You know it's supposed to rain tomorrow but they never know. We might go fishing this evening.

-That sounds fun. Where are you going to fish?

-Just up at the lake.

-Oh, that sounds like fun Mr. Smith. Well, listen, I don't want to take up too much of your time today, but a house on your road sold just last week and I didn't know if there was anything I could do for you at this time?

-Hey, that's good that that house sold. Thank you for the information. I don't think there is anything you can help us with now, but thanks for your call.

-Oh, no problem Mr. Smith. Thank you for your time today. Let me ask you: Is there an agent in the area who you have a relationship with already?

-Well, we have talked to a few, but do not really have a relationship with any of them.

-I see. Well, one day you will decide to buy or sell, and I would like the opportunity to work with you when that day comes. Would it be ok if I stayed in touch with you via email?

-Absolutely, please stay in touch.

-Great! What is your email address?

-mrsmith@abc.com

-Thank you, Mr. Smith. Hey, would you be available for lunch one day soon? I would like to put a face with the name and get to know each other a little better.

-Absolutely.

-Okay, thanks Mr. Smith. I will talk with you soon. Have a good day.

~~~

Of course, that is just one example, but it demonstrates the **main elements of the call**, which include:

- Identifying the prospect

- Introducing one's self

- Asking how they are doing

- Chatting about the weather

- Transitioning to…

- Giving the Reason for the call

- Seeing where the conversation goes

- Identify if they already have an agent

- Get their email address

- Ask them to lunch

This is my bread and butter when it comes to making calls. You can use this script for any type of call. You can use it for cold calls, expired listings, FSBO's, friends, family, etc. This is a great conversation and relationship starter. I have built my entire business on this model.

When you think about the nature of this call script, you will find that it is everything that you want your reputation to embody. It presents you as hard-working, honest, easy to deal with and low-pressure—all in one phone call. Take this and use it. It is very powerful.

Also, if you do not get an answer, always leave a voicemail. Just say something like this: "Hey, Mr. Jones, this is Ricky Carruth with RE/MAX. If you could, give me a call back when you get a chance at 555-555-5555."

Chances are they will not call you back. But they do hear your name on the message when they delete it. So if they hear your name, see your signs and get your mail-outs, you may eventually win them over.

As you are making calls, you are not only finding clients, you are also learning how to make better calls! During this time, you will be creating long-term relationships and build a strong business. So don't hesitate. Get on the phone. The more calls you make, the more confidence you will have. Practice your scripts with other agents. Overcome your fears by increasing your skills and confidence. If you follow the recipe here, there will come a time when your confidence and skills will overwhelm any fear you had and a million-dollar agent will emerge.

6: Organize Your Business and Goals

✳Staying organized will help make you a lot of money. ✳ Everyone has his or her own method of staying organized—some effective, some not. I know it's tough to keep organization as a high priority with so many other responsibilities to juggle. But being organized is the key to not dropping those juggled responsibilities.

✳If you want to become a top producer, you must schedule time to keep all your deals, clients and errands organized.✳ Take 15 minutes every morning and every afternoon to sit down and make notes of everything going on in your business along with your short and long-term goals. That way it's always fresh on your mind.

The way I begin my daily organization is this: I take a fresh sheet of paper and make a list of who I need to follow-up with, what contracts I am negotiating, the deals I currently have under contract, upcoming listings, seller/buyer appointments, errands I need to run, any meetings I have with my team, goals, etc. I write all of this twice a day, adding and crossing off items as they are completed✳I find that the power of writing notes daily about my current business keeps me more engaged with the day-to-day activities I need to be focused on to achieve my goals.✳

✳I also have a daily planner to keep up with appointments and other sales activities I need to be aware of that fall on particular days.✦Some agents keep their notes on their phone or online. Whichever way works best for you is what you should do. The main point here is to start organizing and prioritizing (which go hand-in-hand).

✳**Organization** is the first step towards execution.✦ Organization is how you know what needs to be done.
✳**Prioritizing** is deciding in which order to execute each activity.

These two work together with **Goal-Setting** (discussed below) and **Scheduling**: arranging activities with your calendar/planner.

How do you determine priorities? Each chapter in this book gives you plenty of detailed ideas (such as, for real estate, spending time on the phone is a high priority). And in general terms, we have already said that time management must be a priority. As Rory Vader, author of *Procrastinate on Purpose*, says, "Spend time on the things today that save you time tomorrow." So being organized is itself a priority.

The time I spend organizing my day and week saves me tons of time when I begin to execute on my plans later, which thus multiplies my time. I know exactly what I have to do and in what order to do it. This way I just take care of each activity one after another. This is another secret of how I get so much done. Agents who fail to organize and plan have no direction and thus are just floating in the wind. Floating in the wind with no organization is—to change metaphors—like driving in a foreign country with no road map. You are totally lost. Instead, think of your written plans and goals as a road map that takes you on the most direct route to your desired destination in the time projected.

If organization is your weakness, add to the tips in this book by studying one of the many popular books on organizing, time-prioritizing, goal-setting and project management skills. Read online reviews to find a book that readers rate as concise and effective and proven useful for real-world business practices. (For example, Winston's *The Organized Executive* and Blanchard's *One Minute Manager* are older classics in the genre.) Since my book is not primarily about the details of organization, I leave that to those kinds of self-help/business advice books.

Prioritizing and Goal-Setting: Our long-term goals should give shape and clarity to our priorities. Goals are essential to success. Someone once said that the difference between a **pipedream** (which never comes true) versus a true **goal** is that goals are *written down.* There is power in writing things down, whether it's your **short-term, mid-term or long-term goals** All three types should be written down or they will be forgotten pipedreams. It seems obvious that written goals have a 99% better chance of getting accomplished than just an unwritten, fleeting thought... yet few people actually write down their goals! This is not just my opinion. A variety of psychological studies and surveys have proven that the difference between a written goal and a vague "I oughta do such and such" is like night and day. Done vs. none. Several of those studies also show that goals with *timelines and deadlines* are far more effective tools for success.

Short-term goals can be something as simple as your daily "To-Do List." These goals are the most specific and often have a clear deadline: Do This Today. And if your daily "to-do's" are actually a written list on your desk (or your refrigerator, for personal to-do's), **they tend to get done**. Right? If it is not written down, it may eventually get done, but probably a week from now when you happen to remember it—which is sometimes too late.

Mid-term goals are the bridge between daily To-Do and Long-term goals. Long-term goals are our destination on the map; mid-term goals are the roads to that destination; daily To-Do lists are the individual traffic lights, stop signs, turns and gas station stops along the way. Put another way, without mid-term goals, our daily tasks have no connection to our long-term goals and take us meandering around the countryside, wasting time. With that said, you can see that organizing, prioritizing, scheduling and goal-setting are all intertwined. To be successful, you can't have one without the others.

This means that our big Long-Term Goals still come back down to the little things we do today. And being efficient in those little things requires being organized. No matter how organized (or disorganized) you may be, you can always improve the skill. Remember, being "OCD" — compulsively nit-picky and over-organizing your paper clips by color and size— is not the goal. Use only as much organization as you need to speed up your work; if your time spent purely on organizing is slowing down your work, you are probably missing the point. Keep it simple. ✵Take a few minutes each month to set or adjust your broad goals. Take a few minutes at the beginning and end of each day to sit down and go through your immediate business and find the best way to stay organized on the details. Then get back to executing on those details and making money.

7: Building Referrals

You hear all kinds of sales training about how to build your business on the referrals of your friends, family and past clients. It's everywhere, right? Well, when was the last time someone actually asked you to refer someone to their company? It doesn't happen very often. Despite ample training on how to get referrals, not many salespeople take advantage of it. I see this especially with real estate agents. Most agents do not ask for referrals... and therefore get few, or none. Conversely, the few agents that I do see consistently asking for referrals do extremely well in this department.

＊Designing your business to obtain more referrals is a skill that if done right can bring your business to the next level. Referrals may be the one thing that your business could be missing to reach your goals. To start getting referrals, you must be referral-minded from the very beginning of any relationship or transaction with a client. There are two main ingredients involved in building a referral-based business. They are:

I. You must ask for referrals.

II. You must prove to the person you are asking a referral from that you are the best in the business.

Without both ingredients, you will be missing out on lots of business. Let's break each of these ingredients down one at a time.

I. You must ask for referrals!

If you don't ask for referrals, how will your clients know to give you referrals? If a person is not asked about something, they will most likely never think about it. As an agent, you should never assume that your client already knows you want referrals.

Chances are high that they either know of someone looking to buy or sell right this second, or will be in the near future. They just aren't thinking about relating that to you because they are so involved in their own affairs. One simple thing changes that: ask them to name any friends or relatives who are looking to buy or sell. Then their mind starts to think of possibilities. Suddenly they start giving you names and phone numbers. This doesn't happen every time, but without asking you will never know.

✳The best time to ask for referrals is while you are under contract with a client. When a client is in the middle of a deal, they are more real estate minded. They notice more about the market and strike up more conversations about real estate than they would if they weren't in the middle of a deal. It's like when someone is buying a new vehicle... let's say it's a red car. While they are shopping for a new car, they will notice every single red car that passes them on the road and talk to anyone who they see with one. Red cars are on their mind and they can't help but notice every time one goes by. Then after 2-3 weeks, life goes back to normal and they don't notice red cars as much.

That's the same train of thought that a person has when they are in the middle of buying a property. Real estate is on their mind more than ever and they are talking and asking questions to just about everyone they see about it. So obviously, it's the best time to ask them for a referral.

From the beginning of the relationship until 60 days after the closing, ask them whom they know that might be interested in buying/selling real estate soon. But it's key *how* you word it. Be specific. Make sure to ask them, "Who do you know. ✳" instead of "*Do you know anyone....*" *Who you know* implies that they need to come up with some names. *Do you know* only asks for a yes or no answer...

60

and "no" is usually the quick reflex. We want *names* of potential buyers and sellers.

Plant the seed early in their mind that you love to work on a referral basis and that you will offer anyone they send to you the same great service they are now receiving. Don't ask them too often—but do ask more than once. You will know when the best time is or isn't.

After a Closing, be sure to stay in touch over the next 30-60 days to capitalize on possible referrals they might run into. Let your client know how much you value them, and that if they know anyone else that could benefit from the same service you provided them, you will be more than happy to accommodate. So, get out there and ask for referrals and ask often. You will be surprised at how much business you have been missing out on.

II. You must prove to the person you are asking a referral from that you are the best in the business

The second part of the referral equation depends on your excellence as an agent. To prove to clients that you are the best agent for their referrals, follow these ten principles:

1. Do what you say you are going to do when you said you would do it.

2. Always look professional and wear nice clothes.

3. Build a reputation as the hardest working agent in your office.

4. Stay on top of the active listings and recent sales in the area.

5. Always answer your phone.

6. Be on-call 24/7 for any of your client's needs (including helping them move a piece of furniture).

7. Protect your client's interests always, especially when negotiating a contract.

8. Never answer questions unless you know the answer. If you don't know, reply "But I'll find out," and always find the answers promptly.

9. Listen more and talk less. (80/20 rule)

10. Maintain high levels of energy and optimism.

These ten tips will not only help prove that you are the best in the business, they will also help you *be* the best in the business. If you demonstrate these traits while asking your clients for referrals, then of course they will be happy to send prospects your way. If they know you are flawlessly dependable, they will feel confident in sending you their friends. People will not recommend a business if they doubt its service is reliable. Basically, the harder you work at the fundamentals of being a real estate agent, the better chances you have of receiving the referrals you ask for.

If anyone thinks highly enough of you to send you a referral, respond with the highest form of gratitude. Even if the person they send you spends days and days and never buys anything, you will still be grateful and treat them like family. Let the person who gave you the referral know how much you appreciate the business (even if, technically, no dollar-business happened). Send them a small gift. This will keep the referrals coming strong. Nothing pleases someone more than when they refer someone to an agent and that agent goes above and beyond to help them. It makes them feel like they made the right decision sending friends to a trustworthy agent. People care greatly about their reputation, so make sure you confirm their trust in you. Then they will continue sending you prospects. ✻ Success follows trust and dependability.✻

8: Champions are Made in the Off-Season

"During the off-season when you see other people playing in the Super Bowl, you wonder, and say to yourself, "Are you ever gonna get there and see what it feels like?" And it pushes you a little harder during that off-season to work to try to get there the following year."

~Walter Payton, NFL Hall of Fame

In my market, summertime is our busy season. We make most of our yearly income during the summer months, and in the winter, the market here in my beach community tends to slow down. Your location and market may be different, but almost every real estate market in the world is seasonal in its own way. There are busy times and slow times. Most agents slack back and take it easy when business is slower. Which season do you think I **grow** my business in each year? I'll give you a hint. You cannot concentrate on growing your business when you're busy. That's right, I grow my business in the slow season. Which I refer to as the *off-season*, mindful of the old sports quote, "Champions are made in the off-season!" I live by this quote every year.

Other agents think I am crazy, but I love the slow time of the year. It gives me time to take a deep breath, focus on where my business is and where its headed, and consider what actions I need to take to help it grow before the next busy season. When the market starts slowing down, that's when I pick it up a notch and get to work. People ask all the time, "Been staying busy, Ricky?" And I always have the same answer regardless of the calendar or how hot the market is or isn't: "Oh yes! Slammed!"

I can say that honestly, because even when the market is slow I am still coming into the office at the same time with the same level of energy and drive. I work just as hard or harder in the off-season than I do in the summer.

63

I take this time to reconnect with all my past clients as well as start major marketing campaigns for new clients. My theory is that if you enter each busy season with more clients then you had the previous year, then you should do more business each year. This has been true every year since I began applying this technique. If you will take this idea and use it, you will leave your competition in the dust. No one will be able to keep up with you.

There are pros and cons to each business cycle. During the busy cycle, you don't have time to grow your business and database, but you make more money. During the slow cycle, you have plenty of time to grow your business, but you make less money. Take advantage of the opportunity both cycles present. Realize how valuable each cycle is to the other, and maximize your results in both.

Understanding this concept and being skilled enough to apply this technique will produce a huge positive impact on your future earnings. I went from $150,000 one year to over $400,000 the very next year just by continuing to work when things got slow. Around August, when sales start to slow down for me, I shift gears into "prospecting mode." This is the tricky part for low-producers: recognizing when the season is turning and changing your day-to-day tasks. Don't get caught up in doing the same exact activities throughout the entire year.

When the season slows down, first I identify who my past clients are and what clients I would like to have. Then, over the next few months, I prospect with intensity. Normally, the off-season lasts about 6 months. So, during that time, I try to connect by phone and by getting several pieces of mail in their hand before the next busy season. Once the season is over and sales pick back up, I am too busy selling to focus on those kinds of activities; I return to reaping my harvest from the seeds I had planted all winter long. This technique keeps me busy and productive all year.

My business grows significantly each year, and I make sales during the slow cycle that I wouldn't have made otherwise.

I am now starting to create larger sales goals for the slower months. Although the goals for the peak months are much larger, raising the bar in the off-season pushes me to sell more throughout the year.

If you are not sure which times of the year are busier and which are quieter, ask a veteran agent near you. Then, as part of your planning, goal-setting and organizing, take some time to develop a list of concrete actions you can take during your off-season(s). Your area may even have two or three "down-times" in the calendar year. Whatever the case, put a plan in place for each month, and after time goes by, re-evaluate and adjust the plan for next year.

The philosophy of working harder in the off-season and switching from sales to prospecting is another big part of my success. I look forward to both times of year as I continue to grow my business. Keep in mind that I plant seeds (prospecting) all year long. In the summer, I may only have time to prospect for two days a week. In the winter, however, I get to prospect three or fours days a week. Going with the flow of the seasons in your market and knowing when to switch from selling to prospecting, and vice versa, will allow you to create more business than you ever dreamed you could produce.

Section III: Maintaining High Production

9: Positive Thinking

"Success comes to those who become success conscious."
~Napoleon Hill, best-selling author

The way we perceive situations is generally the way the situation will end up. If you start working out at the gym and tell yourself, "I don't think I can do this," you are right! You probably can't… or at least, you won't. You then did not do the exercises you should have, or if you did, you didn't do them correctly… and you already planted the seeds of procrastination for next time. On the other hand, if you walked into the gym with a positive attitude, saying, "This is so good for me. I can do this!" —then you more than likely did the workout and finished strong. You should believe in yourself and have faith that if you do the activities that you are supposed to do, you will be successful. Belief makes all the difference.

I always envisioned myself as a millionaire. Even when I was a little kid, I expected success. I grew up middle class and worked tough, fixed-wage jobs growing up… but I never gave up on my dreams to be rich. Well, it didn't happen overnight, but I continued working at it and believing I could achieve it. And because I believed with such optimism, eventually it happened.

Having attained my childhood goal, it would have been okay to stop there. But I prefer to stay in the game, as I enjoy chasing the next goal, like the game of cat and mouse. I upgraded my goals and continued pushing forward, always keeping an ultra-positive outlook.

Goals should not be merely monetary. Riches do not equal money. Riches include health, family, happiness, friends, and more.

We speak in this book about money and sales-results because, after all, this is a book about business success. But many of the principles herein also work for attaining other—non-materialistic—goals. Positive thinking can be used in *every* aspect of your life.

Here again, in order to keep this book pithy and to the point, I recommend many of the other books on positive thinking. The old classic, *Think and Grow Rich*, by Napoleon Hill, lays out the proven principles of belief and positive thinking as key to achieving any and all forms of success. Hill famously said, ✻"Whatever the mind of man can conceive and believe, it can achieve." ✻Across the centuries, he is only one of many wise men who have discovered that **positive thinking** is absolutely essential to extraordinary success.

As an example, let's apply this to our topic of real estate success. When you have a deal that looks like it might fall through, stay optimistic about the situation. When you talk about these types of deals to others, tell them, "Yeah, the deal has some hurdles, but it is going to work out." Now you've reprogrammed your brain: rather than your brain accepting a definite failure, your subconscious mind has been told (by your own voice!) to keep working on the possibility of success.

The fact is this: some deals work out and some don't. You have little power after you have exhausted all your resources to make it happen. But a negative attitude jumps *too early* to the conclusion that all has been exhausted. ✻Keep a positive attitude the entire time and you increase your chances of stumbling on a solution.

If a deal truly ends up being out of your control, and fails, your upbeat attitude has still not been for naught: the people around you enjoy being around a positive person (which will pay-off with future business).

At the very least, a positive attitude costs nothing and makes for a happier mind.

Take a look at any group of 100 highly-successful people in any industry. Perhaps *one* of them hit the Lottery or inherited a dead uncle's fortune. But for 90 out of the 100, you will find their success came because of attitudes and actions they had embraced from day one. The vast majority maintained a positive outlook overall, and most of them had that same positive mentality from the start. They always knew they were going to be great and had a definite, optimistic attitude even before they experienced success. And the remaining few may have started out as pessimists and procrastinators, but they will quickly tell you of a turning point in their life, when they discovered the power of positive thinking later in life. They will still credit that change of mind/attitude as the spark for their success. Okay, I made up those numbers but they are not far from the actual "success percentages" based on real-life surveys and studies.

Now, let's look at a different group: non-producers in the real estate industry. This group has a negative outlook most of the time. They have a hard time finding anything positive to think or talk about. These types of agents are easy to spot a mile away. They complain about everything. They make excuses constantly. They always blame someone else for their misfortune. These are all signs of an agent who has low production and who will never break through their own barriers unless and until they have a moment of clarity and change their thought process.

Let me make something very clear. Everything that happens to you in your life, good or bad, is the result of the decisions you made. Sure, occasionally bad things happen. Winners also have bad things happen—they just choose to respond with a positive, "This is momentarily bad but I won't quit" attitude. There is no one else on planet earth that you can blame for your successes or misfortunes. Take responsibility for where you are in life every day.

Dwelling on something bad that has happened to you and blaming others for it only takes you backwards. Remember, there are only two directions you can travel in life. Your life is either getting better, or it is getting worse. There is rarely any in-between. So, let's make sure our lives are going in the direction we want to go, the direction of onward and upward, bigger and better.

Successful people learn from their past, focus on the present and create their future. Unsuccessful people dwell on the past so they can't focus on the present, nor create a future. Think of your life and your business as a river. A river has fresh, new water constantly flowing through, cleaning any stagnant, nasty water out. A negative persons' life is like a swamp instead of a river: the same ole water that has been there forever, stagnant. Nothing new goes on in a swamp—no new water, no movement or flow, the same ideas and thoughts, yielding the same clouded result each time. Let's be a river with a constant supply of new positive ideas and progressively better results as time goes on and moving to a new, clear destination. Be a River!

Chapter 10: Does Anyone Know Who You Are?

There is one thing in this world that no one can ever take away from you. They can take your car, house, and pride, but they can never take away your *name*. Your name is the one gift from the world that you can never be stripped of. Use it to your benefit. Build a brand and sterling reputation around your name. Your name should be synonymous with the hardest working agent in the area, the one who always does what they say they are going to do.

When people hear your name, what do they think of? Ask yourself this question and write down ten answers. Next, make another list of what you *want* people to think of when they hear your name. Then, write a third list of actions you can take that will help you build that reputation. Start making decisions and taking the actions needed to make that second list come true. Brand yourself as an expert in your market. You want people to think of you every time they hear anything about real estate. Dominate your market.

Self-promotion is the use of your name and achievements to advertise and market yourself. When you sell a property, let the world know about it. Send postcards, letters, emails and make phone calls telling everyone about the property you just sold. Promote, contact, post, announce, mail— these words must be part of your daily thoughts.

Every time I get a listing or close a sale, I send a postcard to the surrounding owners about the transaction. Use it as a tool and a reason to make contact. Nothing is easier than calling a property owner and telling them that you just sold a property, followed by the question: "Is there anything I can do for you?" At the end of the year, send out marketing information about how many properties you sold that year. Include the reminder that you are always at their service and will be happy to assist them as well.

*Testimonials are a huge part of self-promotion that most agents overlook. Testimonials are especially powerful in our technology-driven world. Anyone can look you up with the click of a button and read any reviews that might be available. These days, most people will look online before doing any kind of business or purchase: staying at a hotel, eating at a restaurant, hiring a lawyer, and even what real estate agent they should use. Your reputation is more of a factor in today's world than it has ever been in history.

Do your best to preserve your reputable name. Be careful not to lose your cool and say the wrong things in the middle of heated situations. Maintain professionalism always, even when it's not easy. This goes for how you respond to clients *and* agents. You are a team with all the local agents within your area. You are all working together—and will for years to come. If a situation happens that upsets you, take a few minutes to cool off before talking to anyone about it. Come to your senses and figure out what the best way is to handle it professionally. You can't afford any negative publicity.

One "losing your cool" incident may end up posted somewhere online where potential clients can read about it. If they do find it and get a bad feeling about you, it will cost you business. Conversely, the more positive feedback that is posted about you, the better. Just as you have been actively asking people to give your referrals, likewise be forthright in asking people to post positive feedback about you wherever/whenever they can.

So let's focus on getting positive publicity. There are many avenues to acquiring great testimonials. The method I use is to ask a client who had a wonderful experience to email me a brief, positive testimonial. Then I copy and paste that testimonial on my "Testimonials" page on my website.

Potential buyers and sellers can go to my website and pull up the impressive list of all the testimonials clients have sent me over the years. This helps significantly when someone is trying to decide if I am the right agent for them. Clients tell me all the time that they read my testimonial page before calling me.

If you are just beginning as a realtor, even without a single sale under your belt, you can still put general references/testimonials on your website. You can ask friends, former co-workers or business acquaintances to write a sentence or two about what a great person you are, praising your honesty, friendliness, skills, etc.

There are many other ways of getting and posting testimonials. You can use *Trulia* and *Zillow*. These websites are the largest public real estate search engines out there, and they offer an "Agent Profile" that your clients can view—and can use to leave testimonials. Another platform for this is Facebook. A client can post an incredible testimonial on their own wall and tag you. This is a great tool because all your friends and the client's friends will see it. And it's free. You can then also post a link to the Facebook testimonial on your website as well.

There are many ways to obtain and use testimonials to help grow your business. Don't be another agent failing to take advantage of this opportunity to show the world how honest, helpful and effective you are.

Chapter 11: Hiring an Assistant

✸"Better a diamond with a flaw than a pebble without."

~Confucius

Yᴏᴜ might have asked yourself at some point, "How do the top producers handle all of those deals?" There is so much work and detail to keep up with on every single transaction. Then there are all the other duties an agent is responsible for. How do they get it all done—effortlessly, it seems? I will tell you how.✸*Behind every top producer is a great assistant.*✸There is absolutely no way to be a true top producer without an assistant. A huge part of being successful in this business is not only knowing what you need to do but also knowing what *not* to do... or to put it more precisely, what to delegate.

✸Most agents get caught up in a web of activities that don't make them money. To find time to complete all of your essential income-productive activities, you must delegate everything else. Thus,✸being able to determine what the income-producing activities are, and establishing your priorities vs. delegated matters, is vital in the climb to the top of the mountain of success.✸Since I hired and learned how to efficiently use an assistant, my income has tripled, and continues to increase every year.

You will know when it's time to hire an assistant. Your business will become too overwhelming for you to handle alone. There is no exact measure of when that will be, but let me tell you when I decided it was time for me to hire an assistant.✸It was when I started to maintain thirty concurrent listings.✸Thirty was the magic number for me that marked my business load as overwhelming.✸I was getting so many calls from agents asking to show my listings that I couldn't keep up. Not to mention how much it was cutting into my prospecting time and other duties.

❋ I had finally decided that answering all the requests to show was not income-productive. While setting up agents to show my listings to their clients *is* important and must be done right, it can still be delegated. So, I recognized the benefits of hiring someone to handle this. I thought, "If I can take this one task off my shoulders, it will free up enough time to continue chasing more business." It worked. I then started thinking of many other tasks that could be safely delegated, saving me even more time. Here are some on my ❋"Can Be Handed to the Assistant❋ list that might work for you:

- Putting properties into MLS

- Taking pictures of new listings

- Placing signs and lockboxes on listings

- Looking up phone numbers for prospecting

- Sending mailings to my farm areas

- Picking up closing packages from title companies

- Processing paperwork for each deal

- Helping me keep up with details and deadlines of each pending contract

- Getting feedback from each agent who has shown one of my listings.

These are just to name a few. Some agents are hesitant to delegate these tasks to someone else. They have a "If you want it done perfectly, do it yourself" attitude. Listen, I am a perfectionist as well. I felt that everything must be perfect always. But that was one hurdle with myself that I had to get over. I had to be okay with some things just being okay. Nothing will ever be exactly, perfectly right—yet almost everything will work itself out over time. As is often said, ❋"Perfection is the enemy of the good." Let it go!

The main task I first needed to delegate was handling all the showing requests I was receiving, which robbed so much time that I could have spent recruiting new business. For example, when an agent requests to show one of my listings, we first call and see if the property is vacant. With a condo, if it is occupied, the rental company must check with the guests and see if it's okay with them if we show the property during their stay. Finally, we must call the showing agent back and let them know when the property can be shown. It's a process that can become too time-consuming with thirty listings and other tasks to complete. This one task was the initial reason why I hired an assistant.

When I committed to finding an assistant, I wrote an outline of other tasks she could also do to free me up for the income-productive tasks, such as prospecting, following up and negotiating. You should sit down and think about your current business and pick out tasks that you could delegate.*By delegating, you multiply your time. Maybe you aren't ready to take on an assistant right now. Trust me, you will know when it's time. You will have too much to do and feel like you are losing money not getting to the tasks that make you money.

Staying in front of people is what makes you money. Being on the phone, meeting in person, negotiating a contract, showing property, listing appointments… these are the activities that you are responsible for. Everything else could and should be delegated. If you are not yet busy enough to hire an assistant, then set that as a Goal: *"Becoming so busy that I need an assistant."*

The way you achieve that goal is by following my program, making hundreds of calls, sending thousands of mailings and pursuing new business any way you can. Then find your*magic number of listings—maybe it's 15-20 or 30-40. Whatever number you set as a goal, take it as a mission, like your life depends on it. Once you have too much to handle, hire an assistant to delegate all the administrative tasks to and continue your mission to go higher.

Don't slow down once you hire an assistant. At that point, it's time to mash the gas pedal and take advantage of this incredible situation you have put yourself in. Not very many agents make it far enough to hire an assistant. Be thankful that you have made it that far; do not take it for granted. Take it from me, it could all be taken away from you in the blink of an eye. Go to work every day like it's the last day on earth and, as my high school football coach would say, "Leave it all on the field!" Which meant give it everything you have. Don't bring a drop of energy back to the sidelines. Leave every bit on the field. When it's all said and done and you left it all in the office each day and go to sleep that night knowing you did all you could do, you'll dream of the huge success that will shortly follow.

Finding an Assistant

Once you realize you have more work than you can handle and it's hindering your business from growing any further, it's time to find yourself a good assistant. Of course, just as hiring a *good* assistant will grow your business, a *bad* assistant could shrink it. So be very careful when selecting an assistant and make sure you hire one who agrees and aligns with the goals you have for your business. They must understand what the goals are and what their role is in achieving those goals.

You want someone committed to the team long-term, as well. You don't want to hire an assistant who is only looking for a summer gig or for a job until they enter graduate school in the next year. I tell my assistants I am looking for a 5 to 10-year commitment and would like them to stay with me even longer. Many people don't know where they will be a year from now, and are hesitant to commit even to a year.

But in asking for such a long-term relationship, you will get a sense of where the applicant is in life, and in turn, the right applicant may like the idea that this is not a "fly by night" temporary position.

⚹When looking for an assistant, it's good to start by asking the other agents in your office if they know of anyone who might be looking for an administrative position. A referral from a fellow agent is normally a good way to go. If you don't have any luck there, reach out to agents of other offices asking the same question. Most of the time, another agent in the area knows of someone needing a good job. Another option is posting the position on the job finder websites. If you do advertise on one of those websites, make sure to post all of your needs very clearly so that you filter out people who would never fit. The ad could sound like this:

> *Local real estate agent needing an assistant. Must have a strong work ethic with plenty of references, real estate experience, computer skill, and a good personality. Background check required.*

This is a simple ad that will get the phone ringing. I placed a similar ad on *Craigslist* one time and ended up doing two interviews a day for two weeks straight. People are always looking for a job. That gives you options, so take your time and pick the right one. Ask them questions like the following:

- Why aren't you working now?

- What happened at your last job?

- Who are your references?

- If I hired you, do you see yourself working here for the next 5 years? Or: Where do you see yourself in 5 years?

- What are your personal goals?

- Are you planning on getting your real estate license?

- How good are you on a computer and typing speed?

Those are some basic questions I ask a potential assistant during an interview. I also have them fill out an entire application for employment that asks more detailed questions that I review later. I don't get too much into my company or any of my business goals in the first interview. I want to ask them all the questions, narrow my list of potential candidates down, and try to get a good feel of what he or she is looking for in terms of a job.

* After I have had several interviews and a couple of top prospects, I start calling the references they left on their application and all their past employers. By doing this, my top prospects may get narrowed down even further if I find out anything negative from those calls. Once I have a good idea of who my top 2 or 3 candidates are, it's time to bring them back in one at a time for a second interview.

The second interview is actually more of a "trial work day." They will come into my office and work at the job for a day or at least a half-day to see if they will be a good fit. Even then, you won't be able to know absolutely that they fit the position perfectly, but it gives you a much better idea than if you hired them based on the first interview alone.

* In preparation for the second interview/trial work day, you tell them that it is down to two or three candidates and you would like them to tell you and show you why you should pick them for the job. Pay attention to how they work and, in particular, if they were being truthful with you about the skills they claimed in their resume' and/or first interview. You can tell quickly if they know their way around a computer or if they have any real estate experience.

By doing an all-day second interview, you may be saving both of you the heartache of having to fire the person after just one or two weeks after you brought them on board.

⭐Once you have picked your "Finalist," the best person for the job, next bring them in for an orientation of their duties and expectations. During the orientation, you tell them that they will be on a week-to-week hiring probationary period for six weeks. The hiring period is a low commitment period during which, each week, you both re-evaluate the situation and make sure both parties still feel like it's a good fit. If both sides agree that everything is going well and it is still a good fit, you agree to work together another week and then have another meeting.

After six weeks, it's time to sit down with each other and either make a long-term commitment or go our separate ways. If something is not working and can't be resolved, it's nothing personal but the best thing might be to move on and start looking for another candidate. However, if everything went smoothly and you can see this person helping you move your business to the next level, you have found your superstar... and now it's time to start training your new assistant.

Chapter 12: Coaching and Self-Development

I would not be anywhere close to where I am in life without coaching and self-development. At times in your life and career, you will feel like you have hit a brick wall. What has probably happened is that you have plateaued. You have reached a point where you feel like you have learned all you can learn and that you are doing all you can do, yet the results you are after just aren't happening. Then it's time to have faith in the process. Once you have learned the correct actions to take (as in, the same practices of other successful people), you must have faith in the system and keep pounding away at what creates success. The next step in the climb will become clear in due time.

A long journey, a marathon or climbing a mountain— whatever metaphor you pick—all have stages or legs in the process, all require a time to catch your breath before the next step, and all involve developing a thirst! Your plateau may be a time of thirst: a thirst for more knowledge along with a desire to climb higher or at a faster pace. And sometimes you may feel like you can't find relief anywhere. Sometimes the "brick wall" is the point at which you have become dehydrated. That's not *bad*, it just means you are ready for more inspiration, motivation and knowledge, which means it's time for more coaching and self-development. It's time to be quenched.

If you forget to drink water all day because you are too busy, by the end of the day you'll feel sluggish and cranky because of dehydration. With knowledge stagnation, you may get a similar feeling because you became pre-occupied and failed to give yourself the proper rest, reading, coaching and self-development that your mind needs. If you deprive yourself long enough, it will eventually hit you, and suddenly you realize how thirsty you are for more knowledge and help to climb to the next level.

Rather than waiting for that exhausted or "dehydrated" feeling, make it a habit to give yourself a "swig" of coaching or self-development **every day**, and a bigger "swallow" **every month**. Daily, read a book for 15 minutes every morning and play audiobook CD's in your car on the way to and from the office. Anything to keep your thirst for more knowledge and forward-movement satisfied. Monthly or so, look for refreshing workshops/seminars, videos, and real estate company-sponsored continuing education events of a more in-depth sort. And I'm not just plugging my own online courses (although of course I will tell you more about them at the end of this chapter). A wealth of resources surrounds you if you seek them—and many are inexpensive.

Early in my career, I had coaches and fellow agents who wanted to help me. It was great. They taught me things that I still use to this day. I am very grateful for them and everything they did for me. As much as they helped me, ultimately it was up to me to look and ask for help and to act on what I learned from all the coaches and sources. Remember, you are the only one to blame for where you are and where you are going in your life—no one else. So make it happen, no excuses.

Whenever I feel I'm at a brick wall or on a plateau, or that I have learned everything I can, I do one of three things. I either search for a **good book or tape** (CD/mp3) about self-development or real estate that I felt I could learn from, or I go **find a coach** to help push me to the next level. Or at times, it may even require **changing companies/offices** to

a place with higher producing agents with a different set of skills to learn from. So far in my career, I have been with seven different companies. I worked my way up to the highest producing company with all the best agents in my market.

*Being around other high producing agents will force you to step up your game. Healthy competition is very natural; view it as a positive that can boost your income. View competitors as *secret coaches*, learning as much as you can from everyone you meet. I have also had several coaches of a more traditional mentor-type, where I've asked them to formally coach me—in some cases, even *hiring* them to help you succeed. A study by *inman.com* found that 90% of real estate agents who hired a coach increased their income by 10% or more in the first year, and more than half increased their income by over 25%.

Hiring a coach has doubled my business and given me the tools to succeed. There are all kinds of coaches out there that you can find. As a real estate agent, I always selected a coach with a highly successful track record in real estate. Having a real estate coach has given me an enormous upside push in my business.

I now offer affordable personal coaching for real estate agents. Plus, my company, *Zero to Diamond*, offers you an online course that includes assignments, phone scripts, and a 90-Day Action Plan. You can also become a *Zero to Diamond* member, which gives agents a chance to deal directly with me alongside the online course. I will help you determine where your business stands currently, guide you in developing a business plan based on your goals, and hold you accountable to follow through with the plan.

*Coaching is about teaching/guiding, encouraging, AND about holding the "player" to accountability: expecting high performance on the field.

Everyone benefits by being coached, and my online course is a way that you could have a coach without a huge expenditure.

I'm eager to help anyone in whatever way I can, including free presentations I offer from time to time, both in person and on the Internet (including Live Facebook events). At this point, giving back to the real estate community is the least I can do. I am more than happy to answer any questions you may have. I have a passion for helping people. That is what has made me so successful in real estate, and I want to use that passion to help other agents. Go check out the website, **www.ZeroToDiamond.com**. I look forward to helping you.

Chapter 13: The Diamond Life

Ironically, I will never have a "Chapter 13" (i.e. a bankruptcy). Because having a Diamond-level real estate business built upon hard work and smart decisions means I don't have to be a gambler. I am not a real estate speculator or flipper. Do I occasionally invest in real estate? Yes. But my business is not at all rooted in speculation. Whether there is recession or inflation, my business model will bring in a profit and my risk will be low. So let's talk about the good life: the "Diamond Life." Once you have mastered the low pressure, hardworking mindset it takes to be a million-dollar real estate agent, and everything seems to start falling into place, you will get into a good rhythm in your business and your life. This rhythm is special. It will become your happy place. There are a few things you need to know once you hit this level.

One very important thing to remember is to never stop pushing forward and learning new skills. We spoke about a "plateau" as something that is normal and not a bad thing. But if we get permanently stuck on the plateau, it becomes a cesspool of stagnation! The human mind always longs for new refreshment, new ideas and new challenges. Regardless of how successful you become, remember, there are only two directions you can go in life. Make sure you stay the course and continue moving yourself in the correct direction—skyward!

Another important thing to remember is where you came from. I came from very humble beginnings. Hopefully, I will never forget that. I never forget what it took for me to break through the lower-economic middle class and into the upper class. Chances were very low for a guy like me, born without any particular advantage or wealth, but I never quit and I kept a positive mindset always. *Don't take your success for granted.*

Your success can be taken away from you with the snap of a finger. I am speaking from experience. Keep in mind that once you are at the top, you must do everything you can to preserve and cherish it.

A companion word for *cherish* is *gratitude*. It is not enough to attain success; when good things are happening, we should cherish, treasure and enjoy the good times, and that does not happen unless we have an attitude of gratitude. Yes, that's a cliché phrase, but it it's cliché for a reason: it's true. Be grateful for your profession and for whatever level of success you reach. There are thousands of agents who would love to be in your shoes, and chances are that they are out there trying to come up with a plan to surpass you.

The "Zero to Diamond" phrase in this book's title refers to the *Diamond Club* award that RE/MAX gives out every year. Agents receive this award when they have made over $1,000,000 within one year. This is a great achievement for any agent, wouldn't you say? But you don't have to make a million dollars to start living what I call "the Diamond Life." Being honest, diligent and humble, working hard, being a sponge for learning, and having the drive and burning desire to continue to grow—these are the traits of an agent who is living the Diamond Life. If you believe you are a Diamond and you are doing the things that will eventually get you there, then you already *are* a Diamond.

Loving what you do is also HUGE. If you always talk to new prospects with eagerness and do the things that you know you need to be doing with enthusiasm, your work becomes your hobby and tons of fun. I have fun every day because I am at the office putting deals together and making money. It's what I love to do. You must love it or it won't work well for you.

Along with this chapter's topic and the metaphor of a race or climb, let me mention a few more things: health and recharging. Health is wealth. Without it you will not be completely happy with yourself.

Lots of successful people spend their whole lives making money, but having neglected their health, then burn all their money trying to restore their stressed-out health. If you don't take time to be healthy, eventually you will be *forced* to spend the time.

Start becoming healthy today. Get the right amount of rest (not too much, not too little). Eat right and exercise. It's as easy as that. If you are too far down the wrong path when it comes to health, just ease into it. Walk, run, ride a bike, do something every day. Try to eat lots of fruits and vegetables. Today is a good day to start if you haven't already. You will feel better through the day and have more confidence in yourself. Just as with continuing to learn and getting better in your business, you must always continue working on your health as well. Try to get a little better every day with both your diet and exercise. I have been working on my health since 2010 and still improving, still climbing. The fact is that we never get to the top in anything. There is no top. There is only learn and get better. That's it.

As for recharging, it's a must. There is a breaking point for everyone where we can get burnt out. Don't worry, this is natural. The trick is to take a break to recharge before stress harms your body or your work. Taking a break can mean different things for different people. It could be a weekend getaway to your favorite place, or maybe a weeklong vacation out of the country to a place that you have never been before. It could even be just a day or two that you take off from work and take care of things around your house. You must figure out what works best for you. The point is that these breaks are necessary. They give you a chance to forget about work and refresh your mind. I also suggest a good book and meditation when possible. When you return to work from one of these breaks, you feel recharged and ready for action.

Whenever I return from a relaxing trip, I am so motivated that I start selling more than I would have if I had not taken the break. So enjoy your life! One big way to do that is to make your business enjoyable. What's the point if you can't take a trip or some time-off for fun? *Another way that I recharge is by shutting down my business at 5 PM every day (although I do start my day early!). I turn my computer off even if I am not done with my work for the day. Let's be honest, you are never going to be done with work. In this business, you could work 24 hours a day, 7 days a week. You can get burned-out quickly by working into the evening every day.

Allowing work to invade every moment of your life, 24/7, is a recipe for disaster. Sure, answer an email on your phone or take an important call after hours. But outside of your set schedule, only do what must be done. Don't try to continue planning and emailing random people all night. Give yourself nights off. This way you can go home and take care of your home and family life as well. Balancing out home and work is more important than balancing your checkbook!

If you are working with intelligence and intensity, truly doing what you need to be doing from 8 to 5 at the office, you will have no problem feeling good about shutting it down at 5 pm. So, don't live to make "diamonds"; make money so that you can live the Diamond Life. Family, friends, love, joy, peace of mind... that's what matters most—and prioritizing those things does not require you to abandon your business. Again, it's all about a balance of passion for life *and* work. Start the Diamond Life today and you will see what it feels like to have real security and a reason to enjoy every single day of your life.

Conclusion

Thank you for reading my first book. I enjoyed writing it and sharing my thoughts with you about what it takes to succeed in real estate. I hope it has opened your eyes to new ideas that will help you take over the world. This is just the first of many *Zero to Diamond* books and instructional materials I plan to write. Please give me some feedback and a review on how this information helped you.

This business is built on the strength of the relationships you build. Act! Get out there and be the best agent you can be. And don't forget, you can contact me anytime at **www.ZeroToDiamond.com**. I look forward to helping you take your business to the next level and beyond.

Thanks again.

-Ricky Carruth, 2017

Acknowledgements

I want to say thank you to my Mom and Dad for always believing in me regardless of how high I set my goals.

Praise the Lord, who is responsible for all.

Made in the USA
Middletown, DE
04 May 2022

65262952R00055